GOOD FOR THE POOR

D0589115

ETHICS

OUR
CHOICES

Series editor
Canon Stephen Platten

The series aims to introduce specific subjects of concern and controversy within Christian ethics to a wide variety of readers. Each subject is approached at a serious level, but technical language is avoided. Each book should appeal to a wide readership and will be useful in introductory seminary programmes, in programmes for congregational development, and also to individuals seeking information and guidance within their Christian life.

Canon Stephen Platten is the Archbishop of Canterbury's Secretary for Ecumenical Affairs, and Co-Secretary of the Anglican–Roman Catholic International Commission. Previously he was at the Anglican Cathedral in Portsmouth and taught ethics for five years at the Lincoln theological college; he was also Chief Examiner in Ethics for the General Ministerial Examination of the Church of England. He has published in a number of learned journals including *Theology* and the *Anglican Theological Review*. He was Chairman of the Society for the Study of Christian Ethics at its inception, and has been responsible for forging the very close links which exist between that Society and the Society for Christian Ethics in North America.

Already published
Marriage Helen Oppenheimer
Good for the Poor Michael Taylor

Planned titles in the series include
The Morality of Power David Attwood
Women and Ethics Janet Soskice

GOOD
FOR THE POOR

———

Christian Ethics
and
World Development

Michael Taylor

MOWBRAY

Mowbray
A Cassell imprint
Villiers House, 41/47 Strand, London WC2N 5JE, England

© Michael Taylor 1990

First published 1990

British Library Cataloguing in Publication Data
Taylor, Michael H. (Michael Hugh), *1936–*
    Good for the poor.—(Ethics: our choices)
    1 Developing countries. Social conditions. Christian
    viewpoints
    I Title   II Series
    261.8′3

ISBN 0-264-67190-2

Typeset by Colset Pte Ltd, Singapore
Printed and bound in Great Britain by
Biddles Ltd, Guildford and King's Lynn

Contents

Editor's foreword

'The Brangwens shrank from applying their religion to their own immediate actions. They wanted the sense of the eternal and the immortal, not a list of rules for everyday conduct' (D. H. Lawrence, *The Rainbow*). In these two sentences are encapsulated so many of the questions which continue to dominate Christian thought on moral issues. Must Christianity necessarily require of people specific moral responses? Is there a distinctive Christian ethic? How can wider reflections on doctrine be effectively integrated within Christian moral thought? Issues like these and a number of others will be addressed in this series of books, as we focus one by one on a number of topical ethical questions.

A variety of different stimuli converge upon individuals and communities to press home these questions with continuing force at the present time. Technological advancement and medical research both mean that the empirical data with which we must deal in our moral lives change swiftly and often. The increasing diversity of most Western cultures, where many religions, and none, jostle alongside each other, calls out of the moral agent discernment of what his or her religious convictions demand in such a complex world. Changing gender roles and women's issues raise another set of moral challenges. Shifting political attitudes, both internationally (especially within the Eastern bloc) and within nations, contribute yet further patterns of what we might call moral vectors. All of these factors mean that ethical issues are being debated with more liveliness than ever. The multiplication of introductory books on Christian moral theory is a function of this accelerating interest.

Michael Taylor works within the world we have described to ask questions on one of the most pressing issues of our age, that of economic development, particularly among the poorer nations. Starting from basic questions of what the Christian understands by good, he unfolds his argument both clearly and with rigour. This book is thus not an emotional manifesto which appeals to our personal or communal sense of guilt; instead it is a reasoned and passionate discussion of the problems of the Third World, of our responsibilities, and of possible courses of action. It is a real attempt to relate the eternal to the earthly, in seeing what God requires of us in relation to the world's poor.

Stephen Platten

Preface

In this discussion of the ethics of development or, to put it slightly less formally, of our moral duty towards the poor of the earth, I have started rather further back than we often do in such discussions by looking, in Chapter 1, at some of the links between Christian morality and the faith which lies beneath it. In particular I have tried to explain how our moral stances, well-reasoned though they must be, are always to some extent expressions of our faith; and how, in trying to act for the best in the real world, we have to rely to some extent on our faith to interpret what that world is really like: much more dark, for example, and much more promising than we think, and made more fair at much greater cost.

Chapter 2 looks at the moral values we must try, among many other considerations, to be true to in our moral actions. 'Development' itself, highly valued in the middle years of this century, is an obvious example. When we ask how we are to choose between one value and another, including one understanding of development and another, it becomes clear at least to me that we cannot wholly avoid exercising our own judgement despite the limitations and self-interest which inevitably enter in. That in turn is one good reason why we should hesitate to impose our values on others, as Western development has frequently done, and value instead every opportunity to allow others, including the poor, to create and pursue their own values.

Chapter 3 is an attempt—some may say half-hearted—to cut the moralist down to size and face up to the fact that many of the most difficult and pressing decisions in development are not moral but technical: for example, how do you succeed with small-scale agricultural programmes; how do you put an end to soil erosion or make good use of the forest without destroying it; how do you make sure that the considerable though not sufficient flow of 'aid' from North to South is effective; how do you create a viable economy, end the arms race, solve the debt crisis? In such matters moralists may help best by taking a back seat though, not surprisingly, I have something to say about why, even when it comes to technical issues, they should not bow out altogether.

I hope I am well aware that if we are not merely to weep crocodile tears for the poor we need to act on many fronts and tackle issues at many levels ('macro' like the debt and 'micro' like community health care). Chapter 4 concentrates on a single front, however, and explains why I believe we ought to do what we can to strengthen the poor to stand up for themselves against those who, left with the advantage, will decide against the poor in favour of the strong. This somewhat confrontational strategy may seem a long way from Christian ideals, which is why an attempt is made to relate it to forgiveness, generosity, sacrifice and to love.

The final chapter looks less at the content of our moral duty than at its setting in our Christian hope. The record of 'development' is none too reassuring. The numbers of the poor increase. Can we then be sufficiently confident about what can and will be achieved to make sense of our endeavours? I have not attempted to hide my own deep unease at this point nor, I hope, set out to parade it unduly. A Christian believer myself, I haver between settling for a straightforward sense of duty towards the poor, inescapable whatever the outcome, and a confidence, reborn in me as often as not by the poor themselves, that together with God we can make something good out of this sorrowful world.

I have done my best to avoid certain pitfalls in the use of language, notably assuming that gods and mortals are inevitably male when they may not be. Where I have fallen, such as in failing to find a satisfactory way of referring to certain countries and their peoples (Third World, South, developing) that others of us believe have a claim on us and need our help, I have confessed my failure with one exception. The word 'poor' is not only difficult to use about anybody without speedily entering a number of caveats, I have used it almost exclusively of people in the so-called 'Third World' as if similar people with similar problems and opportunities and similar claims on our moral sensitivities and our love did not exist in our own 'First World' not to say on our own doorsteps. That I have done so will, I trust, be understood even if not excused. I cannot deny for one minute that there is an urgent debate, still largely to be had, about poverty in Britain, and for that matter in Europe and elsewhere in the 'North'. I have not engaged in it, not so much because it is a subject entirely discrete from the subject of this book, but because what knowledge and experience I have lies elsewhere.

Not that I have all that much! I have been schooled in Christian ethics but have no professional qualifications in development studies. I have been educated to some extent by the books I have read, but much more at the hands of colleagues in Christian Aid with whom I have been delighted and privileged to work in recent years, and above all by countless communities of women and men I have been able to visit overseas who by their wit and wisdom and faith, despite their suffering, have often made the idea of calling them 'poor' seem completely absurd. I make no excuse, however, for a generalist like myself attempting to bring life and faith together. That is one of the most important tasks for all of us as would-be disciples. Nevertheless, I must record my gratitude to one or two specialists in development, ethics and theology who have commented on my efforts and in so doing have considerably improved them.

My special thanks are due to Stephen Platten for his sound editorial advice and encouragement; to Ronald Preston, who has added to the huge debt I already, gladly, owed him, by reading my manuscript and making many useful suggestions; and to Pam Robertson and Helen Maidlow for typing what I had written with their customary skill and good cheer.

Finally, some may be disappointed to find that in a book about how we ought to behave I have offered little by way of answers to the age-old question: 'what must I do?' Clues abound, but there are no explicit instructions. I have stated my own commitments, but I have not assumed that everybody else's should be the same. There are two reasons for this reticence. First, there are several organizations, CAFOD, Christian Aid, One World Week, Oxfam, World Development Movement among them, who can supply all the help that is needed by those who, recognizing the moral claims of the poor, or better still hearing the promise of the Gospel of the poor, want to get on and do something. Second, I have tried to be true to my own values! I prize very highly a kind of moral self-reliance which, within a community where we are open to the correction of others but are not overwhelmed by them, allows us to judge for ourselves what is good and pursue it. My aim in writing has not, therefore, been to tell others what they should do about the poor of the earth, but to put them in a slightly better position to evaluate what a great many (including the organizations I have just mentioned) are busy telling us to do, and to decide for themselves where their duty lies, and their salvation.

– 1 –

The Gospel and the poor

We met in the Brazilian countryside three hours by road to the west of Salvador. It was so difficult to survive there that many of her family, including her daughter, had left for the city. She remained remarkably cheerful. We had been together to her little church. Apart from the altar adorned with cloths and flowers, candles and pictures, it was plain and simple and reminded me of 'chapels' I knew at home. She belonged to one of the many base Christian communities of Latin America—congregations of the poor which have learnt to tell Bible stories and talk about their daily struggles at one and the same time, and find stimulating connections between the two.

I started making one connection as we travelled together later the same day. Maybe it was a tenuous connection, but it caught my imagination. She was off to visit her daughter Elizabeth. We found her in a city slum, or favela. Life did not seem any easier there than in the countryside, in a tumbledown shack by a dirt road with no 'facilities'. I learnt that Elizabeth was 'with child'. It was not long before Christmas.

I thought of another journey (Luke 1.39–56) when a woman hurried off to another town to visit another Elizabeth—not her daughter but her cousin, and the two women greeted each other and 'the baby moved within her' and they fell to singing and speculating about a time when the hungry would be filled with good things and the poor would be lifted high. The hopes of the two travellers, ancient and modern, seemed to me to have something to do with each other.

When I asked her, however, what stories they turned to in their communities and what connections they made between the Bible and their experience, she did not mention the visit of Mary to Elizabeth. She mentioned the story of Naboth's vineyard (1 Kings 21) and King Ahab's attempts to rob Naboth of his land and Elijah the prophet's stand against injustice and the abuse of power. Land

1

and justice were as important to her and her community as they were to Naboth and his. She also mentioned the story of the Resurrection because, she said, it encouraged them all to believe that one day they would win a better life for themselves and their children. God would keep his promises. Those who hungered after what is right would be filled.

If you were making connections and looking for biblical material to back up your Christian concern for the poor, where would you turn? Would you look with that woman to the prophetic denunciations and warnings of the Old Testament? To its generally enlightened laws providing for the less fortunate members of the community? To the Pastoral Epistles and James's teaching about fine words being matched by deeds? To Paul's energetic efforts to raise funds for the poorer members of the infant Church? Or to the parables of Jesus?

I suspect that the parables will usually win the day and two of them in particular. The story about the Last Judgement and the sorting out of the sheep who feed the hungry from the goats who do not (Matthew 25) will probably come a close second to that of the Good Samaritan who rescues the traveller, robbed, wounded and penniless on the Jericho road (Luke 10). Both would be generally understood, along with almost all the other biblical references, as setting a high moral tone. It is our moral duty to care for the needy.

And there, I believe, we can make an early mistake when trying to understand the connections, as we shall try to do in this chapter, between the poor of the world and our Christianity. We are too quick to see them exclusively and uninspiringly in moral terms. I do not deny that Christians have a moral duty towards the poor, indeed a good deal of this book takes that for granted and goes on to ask not whether such a duty exists but what exactly such a duty might be. Nor do I deny that Bible stories can be used quite properly to remind us of our duty, though to hear in them nothing but moral instruction is probably to underestimate them and fail to hear the alarming and alerting things they have to say not just about our morals but our salvation and where it is to be found.

No, our mistake is that just as in the story of the Good Samaritan the priest and the Levite hurried past on the other side, so we hurry past the proper starting point for any discussion among Christians about the poor; for we are not primarily a people with duties but a people of faith; we are not a moral people but a Gospel people seized first not by the moral Good but by the Good News.

This tendency to hurry past and reduce Christianity to morality is familiar and perennial. It is there in the common assumption that to call someone else a Christian or shyly protest that the adjective does not apply to you, is to comment on the moral quality of a person's life: 'She is good; whereas quite candidly I am not!'. It is there in the way in which Christian preaching rapidly becomes moralizing so that a 'sermon' is scarcely thought of as the announcing of welcome information or 'good news' that many might be glad to hear but as a finger-wagging exercise in telling people what they ought to do.

The same tendency is there, interestingly enough, in the ecumenical movement. Born into modern dress at the beginning of the twentieth century, it has tended to divide itself into two great streams both of which still flow. One is usually called 'Faith and Order', the other 'Life and Work'. It would be too crude to say that one deals with the Gospel and the other with morality, but it is not entirely misleading to say that one has tended to deal with 'belief' and the other with 'practice'. Experience suggests that often we can co-operate in practice where we cannot agree about our faith, so we hurry past. Help for the poor and needy is an excellent case in point. Matters of faith and doctrine may still keep churches apart, but they have long worked together to feed the hungry. Those who do the feeding (the so-called aid agencies for example) show a marked reluctance to have much to say about the Gospel or have anything to do with evangelism. They operate in the moral and practical regions beyond. Gospel territory should be safely left to missionary societies.

It is almost as if, when it comes to practical matters like helping the poor, we operate on a mental map corresponding to the outline plan of Paul's letter to the Romans. If you bracket chapters 9–11 in which Paul ponders the future of his 'natural kinsfolk' (9.3 NEB), the epistle falls into two parts, the first dealing with 'The Gospel according to Paul' and the second with 'Christian Behaviour'. Paul apparently saw a connection between the two, though apart from our behaviour being a grateful response to the good news, the exact nature of the connection is not made evident; but where he saw a connection we tend to see only a transition. We have received the Gospel. We have been won for Christ. We belong to his people. Now we can move on and deal with the practical implications. At which point Gospel things may not quite become the former things which have passed away, but do tend to become the preliminaries or prolegomena now safely left behind.

The relationship between the Gospel and the good can of course be drawn too close. To insist on an abiding and not just passing relationship between Christian faith and moral obligation, in this case to the poor, is not to suggest for example that non-adherents to Christianity as a religion are incapable of doing good. By 'religion' I mean a set of beliefs, about God and Christ, the creation of the world, human nature, sin and salvation and the future; and I mean a set of practices including belonging to a community called the Church, sharing in worship, saying your prayers and studying the Bible as a particularly revealing piece of literature. One outstanding feature of the circles of Third World activists in which I frequently move is that they are full of people who are 'Christians' in both these ways. They believe and they go to church. But the same circles are equally full of people who do not; in fact they seem to attract those who are disillusioned by the Church and find much of what it requires them to believe difficult and unacceptable; yet they retain great respect for the good they believe it stands for and follow after it. My experience of such people—and many others—makes it a nonsense to suggest that only fully paid-up creed-carrying Christians can do good.

Some would strenuously resist such a conclusion. Their faith teaches them that sin goes very deep. Human nature is hopelessly corrupt until touched by God's redeeming work in Christ. We are incapable of doing anything good left to ourselves; indeed one of the most worrying features of our total corruption is the way we hoodwink ourselves and, instead of calling a spade a spade, regard our dubious activities as doing good, when they are not good at all. The charity we offer the poor for example makes us 'feel good' but is of little use to them; and our long-term goals are highly self-centred. Third World countries which, eventually, are able to look after themselves, with good economies and money to spend in the markets of the world, can only benefit the rest of us. What we call 'good' is not good. It can only become so when we are redeemed by the grace of God and cleansed of our ulterior motives through faith or trust in Jesus Christ. Only such committed Christian believers can do good.

Such a neat and tidy theological scheme is difficult if not impossible to relate to the reality on the ground. People cannot be divided up so neatly. Certainly our 'good works' are not so good as we make out, but that is as true of believing Christians as of anyone else. Certainly we need to be touched by those gracious elements in our human experience which make us less pretentious and therefore less damaging, and by those which help us to be more generous and genuinely concerned for another's well-being; but those gracious elements, which I believe are of God and can be found within the Christian tradition, are often ignored by Christian believers as much as by anyone else, and they are never their exclusive possession. The God who made them, made all humankind. The grace that sustains them is common grace and is available to all.

Any insistence then on a close relationship between faith and morals does not imply that only adherents of the Christian religion can do good. Neither am I suggesting that what we believe as Christians points us unerringly towards the good we are supposed to do in the light of it; even less that that good will be distinctive so that Christians will expect to deal with issues of poverty in different ways from everyone else, and so be wary of co-operating with those who are less overtly Christian, or of other religious faiths or of none. The suggestion that Christian Aid and TEAR Fund should not work too closely with Oxfam or Band Aid may sound ridiculous to many as soon as it is made but behind it lies a number of important questions which we shall have to reckon with at some stage in this discussion. In what way, for example, does our Christian faith not only encourage and motivate us to do good but actually tell us what the good is—in this case, what is good for the poor? Do Christians come to much the same conclusions about what to do as everybody else but for different reasons? Can they rejoice that often even the reasons are the same, so bearing witness not to the way that Christians are all too ready to compromise, but to our common humanity under the one God? Are so many of the decisions about what to do for the best so detailed and technical that the broad generalizations of Christian faith do little more than give us a general sense of direction within which several alternative lines of action can be equally acceptable? Is there perfectly legitimate common moral ground between Christians and others, as in these days of multi-faith societies many would profoundly hope? Are there nevertheless occasions when we must make a distinctive contribution, even part company, and if so, how can we recognize them when they arise?

One further point needs making before we try to be more constructive. Far from being desirable some would say that any close tie-up between morals and religion is highly undesirable. Those bent on doing good should not tarry with matters of belief. They are well advised to hurry past! Going back for a moment to the parable of the sheep and the goats, it makes it crystal clear that your eternal future is going to depend on your attitude to the poor. Did you feed the hungry, clothe the naked, visit the prisoner, provide the homeless with shelter? If you did, you are home and dry at God's right hand. If you did not, you are damned. It is true that the characters in the story are surprised by all this. There is a strong suggestion that it is unselfconscious goodness that really counts. But the parable will hardly encourage it in others. Instead it provides a strong and explicit motive for doing good to the poor, and, say the moralists, it is the wrong one: not to save their skin but your own. Religion with its threats and promises, sticks and carrots, punishments and rewards, is no true friend of morality. It leaves a nasty taste in the mouth.

More than that, religious people are prone to a blind obedience that truly moral people tend to despise. They do good under instructions, because they have been told to do it by God. They should surely do it simply because it is good?

THE FAITH OF THE MORALIST

Christians then are not the only people capable of doing good. Their faith provides no easy answers to difficult questions when it comes to detailed practice; it does not often require them to take a different line from everyone else; and it can be a threat to the high-minded morality which quite properly challenges us to seek after good and do it for its own sake. Why then insist that in a discussion about morality we should not hurry past the faith and the Gospel?

One reason which gets overlooked in the debate about morals and religion is that while it is perfectly possible to have morals without the Christian faith, it is not possible to have morals without any faith at all. No moralist can totally by-pass some confession of what he or she believes.

Morality and ethics are about being good and doing good, so that a discussion like this one about the ethics of poverty is concerned to discover and promote what is good for the poor, just as a discussion about the ethics of the penal system would try to get clear what is good for criminals and those who administer their punishment. To take two examples at random, most if not all would agree that it is good for the poor to have an adequate and balanced supply of food and, second, to be self-reliant. What exactly is meant in either case can be debated. How much is 'adequate'? What is 'balanced'? Can anyone be self-reliant? Is it not far better and more realistic to learn to live in mutual dependence? Nevertheless we know roughly what we are talking about and advocating. We certainly know when mothers and children in famine-prone countries are under-nourished, and we do not like it. And we recognize dependency when we see it, where men and women are the helpless recipients of food hand-outs or charitable gifts. It would be good if these people were well fed and even better if they had the opportunity, which often means land, water, seeds and basic tools, to grow the food themselves.

It may seem totally unnecessary to ask why. That is because both an adequate food supply and self-reliance qualify as morally good on one of the most important and familiar grounds in ethics. Almost everyone thinks they are good. They are universal values. They seem so obvious and have such widespread support that they might well be part of an inbred natural morality. Certainly such agreement has to be taken seriously. It is not however foolproof. Majorities, even large majorities, are not always right. We have to find additional reasons for calling something morally good.

A second line of argument is that an adequate food supply and self-reliance are good not just because everyone says so but because they lead to good results. Adequate food ensures good health; it makes life possible; it reduces misery and suffering and aggravation; it sets people free for more fulfilling pursuits such as learning to read or having a festival. Self-reliance may not make you totally independent but it can give you back a sense of your own worth and dignity, the chance to do things your way and not be at everyone else's beck and call, and perhaps of even more importance, the opportunity to make your contribution to the common life, to give as well as take. Both of these 'goods' could have agreeable consequences not only for the individuals who were previously hungry and dependent but for the wider human community; but let us stop there and ask where we have got to in our attempt to answer 'why?'

To some extent we have argued rather lazily that something is good simply because it is not bad. An adequate food supply reduces the misery which results from an inadequate food supply! Self-reliance puts an end to over-reliance on those who cannot always be relied upon. Beyond that we have tended only to push the question back a stage. We have justified one thing by recommending another. Self-reliance is 'good' because it contributes to human dignity which is also 'good'. Food is 'good' because it sustains life which is also 'good'. That process of asking 'why?'—for children an excellent way of putting adults on the spot—can go on for a long time, but eventually it comes to a full stop.

We can justify calling things good by associating them with many other good things, and by offering many good reasons, but eventually we arrive at a point where no more good reasons can be given and we have to take a stand. We think in many ways it is a reasonable stand. It seems to make sense, but we cannot finally justify it. We can only believe it. It is a matter of faith. That may not go for the adequate food supply but it does go for the lives or life that it sustains. It may not go for self-reliance but it does go for the human dignity and self-respect which self-reliance engenders. These are not values we can totally justify so that any sensible person is bound to agree with us. These are values in which we believe.

Such faith is not necessarily a religious faith involving belief in God. The humanist values people very highly. The moralist who prefers us to behave well because we see the point for ourselves and wish to do so rather than because we are under orders, values 'autonomy' or self-motivation very highly. Like adequate food supplies and self-reliance, they may be good to some extent by association. We can see how they lead to other 'goods', but sooner or later we find elements in this network of values which are simply (or mysteriously) good in themselves and where the non-religious moralist and the humanist have to say with everyone else that that is what they believe. Somewhere at the root of moral values are statements of faith, and Christians, when they come to ask what is good for the poor, cannot hurry past and assume they can immediately leave matters of faith behind.

THE REAL NATURE OF THE CASE

We come back to faith yet again by way of one highly practical consideration. Moral action on behalf of the poor or anyone else, however well meaning, will be of no use, and therefore no 'good', if it does not deal with the world as it is rather than the world as we would like it to be or mistakenly assume it to be. If you misjudge a situation you are more than likely to misjudge the action that might improve it and be good for all concerned. Morals have to be realistic.

I think this is one of the most valid points touched on by theories of natural law which, broadly speaking, are attempts to find a basis for our moral judgements not in special revelations but in the ordinary facts and experiences of life available to us all.

Natural law sometimes refers not very helpfully to the moral code which is supposed to be natural to us. We are all born with it as part of our nature or make-up. As human beings we have an innate sense of right and wrong, a law inscribed on our hearts (see for example Romans 2.14). There are certain things which as everyone knows are good or bad. It is common sense. That sounds sensible until you come to ask what these 'certain things' are, at which point the content of the natural law seems rather thin. Alternatively it appears to be made up of attitudes we inherit from our social group without much thought, rather than moral rules that everyone, everywhere, all the time would agree with. On reflection this understanding of natural law seems to get us little further than the observation that human beings appear to be characterized by the capacity to talk meaningfully in terms of 'right' and 'wrong' even though they often argue long and hard as to what is right or wrong on any particular occasion.

More promising is the idea that it is good to understand the nature of things and to act accordingly. To keep the 'natural law' is to do just that. You would not treat a car as if it were a boat, a piece of wood as if it were a piece of plaster, the earth as if it were an inexhaustible energy supply, a patient as if she were a criminal, an animal as if it were a machine, a black man as if he were an animal, a government as if it were a charitable institution. It does no 'good' for any of them.

We must be careful however not to assume that the nature of anything or anyone is always fixed or obvious. There are certainly many features of the world which remain the same. They are part of its welcome stability, and predictability. They give us confidence within which to move. We sometimes call them the laws of nature. Oxygen and hydrogen combined in a certain way and in certain proportions always produce water. The equation $2 + 2$ always equals 4. If you let go of an apple it always falls to the ground. But there are many features of the world which are not so permanent or 'natural'. If you have experienced nothing else they may seem to be, and if on the whole you benefit from them you may wish them to stay that way. Arguments in favour of what is natural then become little more than arguments in favour of the status quo and the status quo is not necessarily the best state of affairs.

These two understandings of natural law—how things always work and how things have been for a long time but need not and should not always remain so—soon run into each other and make moral arguments about right and wrong quite complicated. That is true of contemporary discussions about sexual relations and the family. It will (probably) be always true that you need male sperm and a female egg if there is to be a child; but that children should always be born and reared in two-parent families comprising a mother and a father is not so obvious as once it was, even though it is a long-established and widespread practice and the law of procreation appears to support it. Similar complications enter into debates about the morality of heterosexual, bisexual and homosexual relations.

Not all the arrangements in the world are as permanent or 'natural' as they seem or some would like. That goes for many of the arrangements that affect the lives of the poor. Some have regarded their presence as 'natural', part of the way the world is: 'the poor are always with you', 'the rich man in his castle; the poor man at his gate'. Some races are regarded as naturally not just different but inferior to others. They are considered to be a lower grade of human being, of poorer quality, and to be treated as such. Hence Archbishop Desmond Tutu's call for a new anthropology in South Africa, by which he means a new understanding on the part of whites of the true 'nature' of black people.

Again for some if not most of us there are natural social structures. Many poor people still believe their place is at the bottom of the heap. Many powerful and wealthy nations and social classes believe in their natural right to rule. The majority still regard male supremacy and domination as natural. As a result women are often the poorest and most exploited of all people on earth. Great care has to be taken over calling any pattern of life 'natural' so granting it a seal of approval. Very often it could and should be changed.

Many of these points about what is natural have been raised afresh in the contemporary discussion about caring for the planet and 'Integrity of Creation'. The discussion is of considerable relevance to the poor. We have, it is argued, raped the earth, ruthlessly exploiting its resources and upsetting the delicate balance of nature. We cut down the trees, sometimes unthinkingly for fuel, sometimes greedily for profit, until eventually the rain does not fall. Or we pollute the air so that when the rain does fall it is full of acid and destroys the trees. We over-farm the land until it is exhausted, eroded and infertile. The desert creeps south. Failing to take care of the earth we make it increasingly difficult for the earth to sustain our life. The hungry remain hungry and in parts of Africa for example, where the worst effects of our lack of stewardship coalesce, millions starve and die. We must develop a healthier respect for nature's ways.

There is obvious truth in that. Barren land will never grow food. Waterless crops will never yield a harvest. These are iron laws which cannot be changed. It is also true that nature can be changed quite drastically not only for the worse but for the better. Clearing forests, draining swamps and shutting out the salt waters of the sea is possible and at times necessary to grow food. The desert, with the help of modern technology, need not remain arid but can blossom like the rose. In the past we may have been too quick to interfere but the response is not necessarily a hands-off policy as if nature, left to itself, will look after the human race. Conservation can be a welcome form of stewardship. It can also be a less welcome brand of conservatism that inhibits the inventiveness which is capable of improving the quality of our lives.

Natural law theories then can over-estimate the extent to which the ways of the world are fixed and being good is conforming to the way things are. They do, however, remind us that no good will be done if we disregard the nature of things and of people, or fail to be realistic and deal with the world as it actually is. But why does all this amount to another reason for not hurrying past the faith when we come to consider our moral responsibility for the poor of the world? Because the truth about our world and ourselves, its true nature, what it is really like, is not simply read off from what is all about us and within us.

It is not all obvious if only we pay careful attention to what is before our very eyes. Our experience, observation and research will tell us much. There is much to which many will readily agree. We may agree for example to a number of basic needs which must be met if any of us are to have a chance to be human at all: our need for food and shelter and community and some room to manoeuvre; and some recent natural law theories have appealed to these ordinary and obvious facts of life as pointing rather obviously towards our moral obligations.[1] But there is much to the world that is not just a matter of seeing what is in front of us but of interpreting what we see; and interpretations differ. Just as faith enters into values so that at certain points we can no longer give reasons but have to confess and take a stance, so faith enters into our account of the real nature of things. There comes a point when we cannot demonstrate but only confess what we believe, though just as our 'stand' on certain values does not fly, we hope, in the face of reason, so our interpretative 'beliefs' about the nature of reality do not run counter to the evidence.

SOME GOSPEL REALITIES

The Christian Gospel is one such set of beliefs. It is the result of careful observation of history and reflection on the facts of life, including the fact that Jesus of Nazareth was born and executed, and raised the spirits and hopes of his followers. But it goes beyond the facts. It draws on insights, often given rather than achieved through revealing experiences, most notably the experience of Jesus of Nazareth, his living and his dying, to interpret the facts and make sense of them. The result, though sombre in many respects, is a fundamentally positive view (good news) of what is the nature of the case if God is as God is made out to be by the story of the Jewish Jesus. It has much to say about the kind of world we live in, what kind of people we are, how we and the world are redeemed and made new, and what kind of future is in store for us. It sets out the reality which we are foolish to ignore if we want to do anyone, including the poor, any good.

As we shall need to remind ourselves again later, there may be one Jesus but there are different accounts of him and a whole family of faiths or Gospels that claim to be inspired by him. If I now indicate what Christian faith has to say about some aspects of reality, the 'faith' referred to, though I believe shared by many, had better be understood as my own. I shall leave on one side the

11

affirmations that the material world is good, that our very existence is to be welcomed, and that life is worth living; not because they are unimportant or irrelevant to our present concerns—far from it—but because they are familiar enough. I shall also pass over the idea that God with us can eventually make a new world out of this rather sorry old one. I remember vividly a leader of the Evangelical Church in Ethiopia talking against the background of renewed famine in his country, dry, barren and wounded by war, telling me that 'this land could be heaven'. That was his way of stating the Christian hope that the reality we are dealing with is not beyond redemption. It is a hope to which we must return and discuss at some length.

From a whole range of beliefs, about the created order, sin, human nature, salvation and a present and future Kingdom, I touch on just four. First we tend to be possessive. We regard many things and sometimes people as our own. We speak of 'my belongings', 'my money', 'my children', 'my home', 'my life'. Some regard a home-owning, share-holding, low-taxed democracy as ideal. In all sorts of ways we reveal and insist on our right to dictate what happens to what is ours. For the most part we regard it as quite proper to use it for our benefit. When we do give money away, to the poor and needy for example, we may be glad to give but we are reluctant to let go. We have a strong sense of giving what is ours, of our right to earmark it for a particular use, certainly to receive some account of how it has been spent. Should we disapprove, then we have little hesitation in withdrawing our support.

Doubtless there are good and understandable reasons for much of this. With regard to possessions, it would be highly inconvenient and irritating if, when it came to basic equipment, we never knew who owned what. We need a degree of security. We need some safer territory, like the home which is the castle, where we do not have to compete with all the others but can live with ourselves. What we own often relates to what we have earned. The good Lord may have given us the earth for a possession but it takes a great deal of work before it is of much use to us, and if we have done the work then we believe we deserve to have and enjoy the results. Again, a clear understanding of what I own and of my right to it affords some protection from predators who snatch and grab what they can. Ownership can also foster a sense of responsibility. We tend to look after what is ours better than what is not, and such stewardship is always to be encouraged.

Possessiveness however, justifiable as it may be, especially in a sinful world (another aspect of reality to be taken into account if we are to do any good), can leave us too content with the world as it is, where comparatively few possess so much, and so very many possess little if anything at all. 'What's mine is mine', we tend to feel, especially when the uneven distribution is in our favour. And what of the subversive Gospel idea that we own nothing? We may be responsible for looking after the world and all that is in it as best we can, especially that small part of its immense wealth that falls into our hands; but our tendency to assume the right to dispose of it as we think fit, and largely for our benefit, should be tempered by the realization that it is not ours nor anybody else's.

Such an idea is inspired mainly by the 'givenness' of so much of what we say we own. If we have made our own pile (of money or bricks or whatever), the opportunity to make it, the ability to make it, the raw and refined materials out of which it is made, owe nothing to our efforts at all. The same idea finds some support in the creative if paradoxical experience of those who possessing nothing find themselves possessing all things; and its time appears to come in that most human life of all seen in Jesus. It is curiously fulfilled and finished yet it is characteristically empty-handed, poor, dispossessed, giving all it has rather than keeping anything in reserve, with nowhere to lay his head.

Good may only be done if amid all the complications and ambiguities we act to some extent as if in reality the wealth of the world is common wealth: as if it were given equally to all, deserved and undeserved by all, available for the benefit of all and requiring from all as great a degree of shared responsibility for its use as we can organize.

Second, we have already hinted at a dark and greedy side to human nature which any who seek to do good must take account of. The Gospel believes there is a brighter side as well. When it speaks of us being made in 'the image of God' it points to what it sees as a radical difference between us and all other beings. It is partly a moral difference, not that we are moral and animals for example are immoral, but that we know what it means to be morally good or bad whereas such ideas do not and could not occur to them. To call a dog 'good' is merely to acknowledge that is has done your bidding, not that it has freely chosen to do what it believes to be right.

But the phrase 'made in the image of God' points to something beyond morality. It makes morality possible. It is our ability to think our way out of ourselves; to rise above our current situation; to laugh at it and so detach ourselves from it; to think not just about ourselves as we are, but to imagine what ourselves and others and the circumstances we share might become. This ability to transcend ourselves is complemented by the ability to transform. We do not have to conform to things as they are, we can change them, as indeed human beings have done since our time began. We make history. There is a story to tell, and not simply because we evolve and adjust under pressure, but because we revolt and take the new ways that we choose.

These changes we are capable of imagining and carrying through are not always of course for the better; and in any case human beings have not always thought of themselves in these terms. Sometimes they have conceived of the world as fixed, made in a certain way. Even social arrangements such as classes and hierarchies, high and low, rich and poor, master, mistress and servants, have been seen as the way of the world, reflecting the divine ordering of things. The great virtue has then been unquestioning obedience not restless imagining, and human beings were thought to be true to themselves and their nature by accepting their lot and settling down in the world as they found it.

Just because many now think differently and restlessly interfere with nature and social structures, human life and the most intimate of relationships, imagining and experimenting with what might be, does not mean that that is what we are meant to do, or that that is our true nature as human beings. Facts cannot be translated into values (an 'is' into an 'ought') quite so directly. Nevertheless that is what, as a Christian, I believe. We are made in the image of God, and God is a creator, forever going beyond what is, and making something out of what is not. God is unmasked and revealed most clearly in the marvellous creativity of Jesus, who is not only the first born of a new creation, the harbinger of a new world, but inspires a (religious) movement which is not devoted to maintaining a fixed tradition (beyond the tradition of remembering his creativity) but to turning the world upside down for the better, so that among other things the poor inherit the earth.

Our humanity is exemplified in Jesus, and my experience of him adds confidence to my interpretive belief about our taste for interfering. I believe we are very much ourselves as human beings when we are at our creative best. That is the reality we are dealing with and we are not likely to do good if we fail to take account of it by allowing ourselves or others to be resigned for example to the inevitable, or by being so paternalistic or oppressive that we deny people the space and freedom to make their own choices and their own mistakes. Worse still, we shall do no good if our expectations of others are low, treating them, not least the poor, as if they were merely the objects of history about whom we talk and for whom we plan; rather than the subjects of history brim full of fresh and constructive ideas, as capable of surprising us as we them with creative contributions, people with whom we work and from whom we receive.

A third belief takes me near to the heart of my Christian faith. We have already commented on the creativity of Jesus. He added to what was given and made more of himself; he transformed the lives of many who came into contact with him; he made such a profound difference to the world that many decided it was a new world. How was all this achieved? In many respects he seemed to have little to do with the usual ways to get things done. He did not draw on the more traditional sources of power. He had no influential public position so that he could move events by virtue of his office. He had, as we have said, few possessions and no money to buy his way through. He had no organization to speak of. The small group he recruited seemed perfectly capable of falling apart. He was not well connected. He rejected any idea that he was a ruler in any sense that was familiar to the politicians of the day. He seems to have been popular at times but with no reliable popular base. His home town was something of a joke and in any case rejected him. As to the might of weapons and armies, nothing seems further from the style of a leader who discouraged his followers from fighting, even in self-defence, and who indicated quite dramatically on more than one occasion that he came not as a warrior but in peace. It is not altogether clear that he was even a particularly dominating character. He certainly appears to leave people to make up their own minds and choose their own way rather than lord it over them.

How he achieved what he did remains a mystery, even to the best brains of the Church which have busied themselves for centuries developing theories about 'the work of Christ', none of them entirely satisfying. One or two things however are clear.

There was about the way he worked an outstanding generosity of spirit. He was generous in his treatment of those who were treated generously by almost nobody else. Whole sections of society seem to have been written off or pushed to the margins. They were referred to in dismissive terms such as 'outcasts' and 'sinners' and 'law-breakers'. Some were sick, such as lepers, the mad, the blind and the lame; others immoral, such as harlots, the idle, thieves, robbers and tax collectors. Many, like the poor, were simply unimportant. Jesus repeatedly gives the impression that they are all central to God's concern, part of the human family, sons and daughters of Abraham. He touches and heals them, befriends, forgives and includes. He inspires in them a new sense of their own worth. This generosity even showed signs of breaking through what for most

Jews remained an impenetrable wall of partition. He acknowledged the neighbourly kindness of a Samaritan and the faith of a Gentile.

This generosity showed little concern for the cost or the consequences to himself. He appears to have given away all that he had to give: exercising to the full his gifts of healing and teaching; offering support to those with few if any champions; making himself endlessly available to the crowds which sought him out; caring more about food for others than shelter for himself. Convinced that there was a way, as a servant to the nations, that would lead his people to peace, he gave all that he had to persuade them by word and deed to follow it.

As a result he made enemies as well as friends. Fear and vested interests combined against him, and he did nothing to protect himself. The generosity remained, reflected in the brilliant images of the Sermon on the Mount of those who turn the other cheek, and go the second mile, and give without fuss to those who ask, and love their enemies. Such were the forces that led to his death; and such is the way of working that turns out to be so miraculously creative that it raises what is dead to life. It can be summed up in the more familiar and more formal language of love, forgiveness, self-emptying, vulnerability, suffering and sacrifice.

At the heart of faith is this man and this suggestion that, when it comes to it, this in actual fact is how good is achieved. I believe it has to be reckoned with over and over again when another kind of realism suggests that, given the world we have, good can only be achieved in rather different ways.

It would be misleading to give the impression that I am always sure about what to believe. For example we have touched on the more perverse side of our human nature. But to what extent it is in fact perverse, wilfully going against what it knows to be right, and to what extent it is fearful and insecure, the victim rather than the perpetrator of hostile circumstances, I am not sure.

Christian tradition has often talked about a reality even more alarming than our perversity. Paul (in Ephesians 6) claims we are not up against flesh and blood but 'principalities and powers'. In so doing he accurately reflects the universal experience of forces at work, usually (we feel) against us, that are far bigger than any of us and sometimes than all of us put together. They soon make their presence felt should anyone be interested in a better deal for the poor. They come in the shape of big business interests, trans-nationals, economic and market forces, political imperialism, oppression and military might. They threaten to destroy the planet.

These powers are not only characterized by size and strength and influence, they are surrounded by an air of mystery. They are very difficult to control, to stop in their tracks, prevent or change. They apparently have a life of their own. They are an open invitation to mythologize, whereby we give them their own personalities and centres of consciousness. They become spirits and demons and devils, self-conscious, thinking, acting powers and rulers, living on another plane and needing to be dealt with in a quite different way. They will win or be defeated in a cosmic, supernatural war such as sometimes is depicted as surrounding the great struggle of the cross. In that case the heart of the matter is more or less beyond us. It is taken out of our hands. We can do little except have confidence in the eventual outcome and, by witnessing to the power of love, maybe put the fear of God into the powers of this dark world.

Myths of this kind ring true at many points. We do not understand everything. Much remains beyond us. Evil can be so monstrous that there is little else to do but resist rather than reform it and cast it out like a demon. The world is not changed by merely trying to re-arrange it. It has to be redeemed. You have to change its spirit as well as its shape. It needs God more than it needs us.

That having been said, the de-mythologizers also have a point to make. What is the reality? Turning powers into personalities may be an acceptable way of saying that we do not understand everything. It must not become a way of denying that we can understand a great deal more if only we try, or provide an excuse for deputing to a remote God what is to be achieved by co-operating with an incarnate God who is near at hand. We must not settle for a mystery to solve a mystery. Mystery and understanding may often grow together but that is no reason for not increasing understanding.

Is it really true that the powers of this world have lives of their own and are beyond control, or can we understand the reasons why collective greed, or belligerence, or whatever, become so strong, defensive and virtually unstoppable? Can no one ever know how huge and complicated systems work and so modify them for the better? Can we not go on from Christ to learn more and more of what really makes for a creative difference in human affairs so that we not only bear witness to him or tell his story, or preach to the powers of this world, but work in ways inspired by his to turn them to good?

If we are to be of any use it would be foolish to suggest that powerful realities we must reckon with are anything but mysterious and strong and full of tremendous energies, but I believe they are still capable of being better understood and tamed until they are more like our servants than our masters.

17

THE GOSPEL OF THE POOR

Having argued that the Gospel is the springboard of our action for the good of the poor, reminding us of our moral duty, offering a sense of values, providing us with insights into the nature of reality, we must face up to the challenge that we do not know what the Gospel is and that only the poor can tell us.

There is a good deal of agreement these days that the Gospel is for the poor. They are not merely part of the follow-up. They are its subject matter. The good news is about their status in God's Kingdom and the reversal of their condition. The proof text is lifted from Isaiah and quoted in Jesus' sermon at Nazareth (Luke 4): The Spirit of the Lord is upon me. He has anointed/appointed me to preach good news to the poor, to open the eyes of the blind, to release the captives, to proclaim the acceptable year of the Lord, which may have been the Jubilee Year when debts were forgiven, land and possessions restored to those who in dire straits had lost them, and slaves were set free.[2]

If something short of a social revolution follows the sermon, the poor and marginalized are clearly the centre of attention. The rich are repeatedly warned. The poor are constantly blessed. Jesus is the friend of outcasts and sinners. He feeds the hungry, promises them the earth for their possession, and is welcomed by those who looked and waited for the day when the mighty would be brought down from their thrones and the humble lifted high. The Gospel is certainly good news for them.

There is perhaps less agreement as to how far this emphasis on the poor should be taken. For example, in the Christian tradition which I know best there is much which would resist it. As a matter of plain historical fact it has long put the emphasis in a different place. Its appeal has been to the middle-class and the comparatively well-off rather than to the poor. It would insist however that there should be no particular emphasis at all. Christ died for all, and all have sinned and come short of the glory of God. The fundamental problem which the Gospel addresses is our disobedience, and our need of forgiveness is as universal as the mercy of God and the invitation to the faith and trust in Him which alone can meet it. The Gospel is not for the poor, or for the rich, or for any one group more than another. The Gospel is for the sinner, and sinners are everywhere, and one sinner's salvation is as good as another's.

There is truth in such arguments, but they are too easily used to justify forms of Christianity which make a home for themselves in favourable social conditions enjoyed by comparatively few (given the numbers of the poor) and startlingly different from those which surrounded Jesus and the earliest Christians.

Rather than resist the Gospel's emphasis on the poor, others find in it a quite definite bias. The Gospel favours the poor; it exercises forms of positive discrimination; it puts the poor first; it gives them priority; but in what sense?

One or two important points can be made briefly. First it is not true that since all are sinners all are equally in need. The needs of the poor are far greater than those of the rich and the comparatively well-off. They have scarcely enough to keep them alive let alone the wherewithal to make the best of their lives. They have poor health, little education, insufficient food and water. Just as regrettable is their lack of opportunity to decide what happens to them. They are not free to be creative. They tend to come rather low down on the agendas of those who make decisions and even then those decisions are rarely in their favour. They need allies and champions. The poor have not heard much good news for a very long time. Natural justice apart from anything else would suggest that they have prior claim.

Second, the poor do not come first because they are more deserving or more virtuous than the rest. As a matter of fact there is, as we know, a fairly widespread assumption that the poor are less deserving and less virtuous than the rest. It existed in the time of Jesus. The poor and the outcast were easily written off as 'sinners'. Today it is often implied that if people are hungry or out of work or diseased, or if countries are 'underdeveloped', it is largely their own fault. To follow Jesus and bless the poor instead of cursing them is not suddenly to become romantic and regard the poor as entirely innocent victims who, doing no wrong, exude an exemplary if previously unsung brand of goodness. They are no better and no worse than the rest. They can exploit, hate, hurt and oppress. They can be as corrupt and perverse (or frightened and insecure) as the better off. All have sinned and come short of God's glory.

Apart from the fundamental question of need, there is another reason why the poor should be paid special attention. The Gospel did not come from the rich and the powerful in the first place. It did not come from Pilate or Herod or the leaders of the Jews but from Jesus, son of Mary and Joseph. That was the direction from which the wind of the spirit originally blew. And it was the poor who heard the Gospel, received and understood it and therefore possessed it and became best placed to offer it back. Maybe they still are.

When John the Baptist's disciples came looking for evidence that Jesus was the promised Messiah (Luke 7), Jesus pointed out that the poor were having the good news preached to them. The implication is not only that the Gospel was being proclaimed but that the poor were hearing and accepting what was being said. They welcomed Jesus and they welcomed the words from his lips and the deeds which made the words ring true.

Again this is not necessarily a case of moral superiority. In many ways the poor were better placed to hear what Jesus had to say. Their position was not being threatened as was that of the rich and the righteous, the established authorities and the powerful. The poor had little to lose and nothing to protect. The Gospel did not sound like a threat but a promise. Again, since they had so little, they were less likely to regard themselves as self-sufficient without need of additional instruction from a new and upstart teacher— hardly a Teacher of the Law! The Bible tends to see a coincidence between poverty and piety, and for this very reason. Those who have little or nothing are more likely to recognize their insufficiency and need and, having little else to rely on, rely on God. The poor had ears to hear. Even the rich can testify that, where their life is under threat, illness and misfortune strike, and we lose too much of what we have, fresh insight can dawn as to what really matters and sustains life. It is more than likely that the poor, whose life is always under threat, can be blessed with even more acute perception.

Outcasts and sinners then were peculiarly well placed to hear the Gospel Jesus preached, and many of them did. The poor may be equally well placed to be the preachers and evangelists from whom we receive the good news today.

Most of us were not brought up to think that way. Christianity and all the good that goes with it tend, in our way of thinking, to move from West to East, North to South, rich to poor, from the one-third world to the two-thirds world. That was true of the historic missionary movements of the European churches and remains true of the flow of aid and technical assistance today. It could well be the deeply-rooted assumption underlying a book like this: 'good for the poor' will come from the likes of us.

Some enlightenment has broken out. The poor for their part are more sceptical of anything good coming out of the rich. The rich occasionally show some awareness of the harm they have done and still do when they assume they know best. Most important for our present purposes is the growing recognition that a clear distinction between rich and poor can soon break down and that the so-called 'poor' have much to give to the 'rich' which the rich in their poverty badly need to receive.

That need can sometimes be acknowledged in a rather condescending way, for example at the level of cultural exchanges which are only tangential to really important issues, where we can admire without being affected. But when it comes to the poor and the Gospel we are nearer to the heart of the matter. We who thought we knew what Christianity was all about must learn it afresh. We who have seen ourselves as the purveyors of Christianity must now learn to receive.

At the level of understanding (if, in the light of what we are being taught, it is appropriate to put it that way) we have begun to hear the voices of the poor in a range of theological writings which, we are told, are the result of listening to and systematizing what the poor have to say. That in itself is something of a jolt. In the past we have tended to turn to a scholarly elite to learn the ways of God. We have not trusted the experience of God's people, or God's own declaration in the incarnation that God is with them and made known to them.

The writings include books of liberation theology, Minjung ('mass of people') theology from among the poor of Korea, black theology rooted in the black experience of slavery and exploitation, feminist theology, theology by the people such as the people of the base Christian communities. Sometimes the style of writing is less formal and systematic such as *The Gospel in Solentiname* by Ernesto Cardenal of Nicaragua. Sometimes it is sharply prophetic as in *The Kairos Document* and *The Road to Damascus*.[3] These voices are increasingly familiar. We must guard against them becoming too familiar. It would be wrong to say they confront us with another Gospel or a different Gospel. They point us back to the Gospel which they believe was first announced by Jesus to the poor. Nevertheless, it can seem like another Gospel when many of its emphases are in sharp contrast to our settled views.

This Gospel according to the Poor announces, for example, that there is to be a great reversal, not a few improvements to things as they are. The last will be first. The humble will be lifted high. Rank outsiders will lead the way into the Kingdom. This Gospel agrees with ours, that the present is not as God intends and that the future will be different, but it insists that God's future is more immediate than we have assumed. It is not merely a dream for dark days to keep up our spirits, or a promise of compensation, or an excuse for counselling patience. It is a present reality, as immediate as an Exodus from Egypt. It is of this world just as much as the next.

This Gospel of the Poor promises peace and reconciliation—it rejoices in forgiveness—but it firmly announces that these have nothing to do with friendly personal relations which leave unfair and oppressive social orders unchanged, or with being co-operative rather than confrontational in the face of injustice. Forgiveness goes with repentance, reconciliation with justice. It is not the peace-keepers who are blessed but those who hunger and thirst after what is right. This Gospel, like ours, promises to teach us truth and that the truth will make us free, but truth will not be readily discovered in the realm of ideas where we argue over doctrines and abstractions and give or withhold our agreement to 'believe' them.

A large part of the truth is clear: God is for the poor. The rest of the truth is unlikely to be known until we have taken the same stand as God, and the poor are as much our practical priority as they are God's. Truth is a guide to obedience. What we think we understand of God's will is a guide to what we should do, but only for as long as obedience is understood to be the main entrance into truth. The arena of truth is action and commitment not mental attitudes, just as salvation has more to do with setting free from actual sets of circumstances than with notional adjustments to our relationship with God which change nothing on the ground. The Gospel of the poor may further remind us that the incarnation is less of an occasion for arguing over the exact nature of Christ's person as God's declaration of how essential and creative it is to stand with and stand by those from whom it seems prudent to keep our distance.

The poor then are anointed/appointed to proclaim good news to us; to open the eyes of the blind. It would be quite misleading however to speak of this only or mainly at the level of 'under-standing'. That would be far too cerebral to be true to the spirit of liberation Christianity. However rigorous the reflection which must follow, the source of this Gospel lies primarily in the experience and life of the poor evangelists.

I recall for example more than one occasion when what I took to be the reality of a situation brought me close to despair. The dry dead bones of a people's suffering could never live. The injustice and oppression could never be reversed. I have felt like that in South Africa and Ethiopia, and among the homeless and the landless of Asia and Latin America. I have come close to it in some communities in Britain. We must return to this theme towards the end of this book, but it is in the same situations and from the same people that I have received the Christian hope which I lacked. Sometimes it came too close to unfounded optimism for my liking, but more often it was a spirited, even joyful form of courage and defiance which would not accommodate or give up in the face of evil and was confident that it would overcome. Where I had thought to bring a measure of hope it was there already to an astonishing degree, and it was I who needed to receive.

In the course of this chapter I have argued that if we are interested in what is good for the poor we should not, as it were, hurry too quickly past the Gospel into the realms of moral debate as if, having given us our mandate, the Gospel was of little further relevance.

It is true, as we shall see later, in our discussion about the effectiveness of our moral actions (Chapter 3), that we can over-estimate the Gospel's contribution to the substance of our moral decisions. We can expect too much of what it has to say, particularly about the details of what we ought to do; but our present concern is with expectations that are far too low. To put it more technically, Christian ethics are theological ethics, drawing deeply on the insights and affirmations of the Gospel and the faith.

To return to where we began, there is a certain irony in the way in which the parable of the sheep and the goats in Matthew 25 is understood almost wholly in moral terms. It is heard as a massive 'ought', firmly pointing us to our moral duty to care for the needs of the poor. We are to feed them, stand by them and grant them refuge, whether we do so through acts of personal kindness, which is the main picture which comes across, or through more organized move-ments for relief and development, peace and justice.

The parable can also be heard however not as a moral sermon but as a proclamation of the Gospel: 'Inasmuch as you did it to one of these, the least of my brothers, you did it to me'. Is that a com-ment on the high moral worth of acts of simple kindness; or is it a broad hint as to where the Christ of God, the agent of our salvation is to be found? Do we go to the poor only to fulfil our moral obliga-tions or to receive whatever we require to negotiate the chasm between life and death, damnation and happiness? And by going to the poor and therefore to the Gospel, do we actually do what is good or, rather, begin to put ourselves in a position to know what the good for us as well as for the poor might be?

– 2 –

The value
of development

Much of the business of morality has to do with what we value as
good for ourselves and good for others, whether rich or poor. A few
of those values seem so far beyond question that they are absolute.
The freedom to have some say in what happens to you and not be
totally controlled and dictated to by everything and everybody else
would be one of them. Truth telling would be another. We may not
always live up to them. In exceptional circumstances, we may
deliberately qualify or appear to disregard them; but the very fact
that when we do, we feel bound to defend our actions and explain
ourselves proves that their status as values remains untouched.

Even when they are not absolute, many of our values are rarely
questioned. It could hardly be otherwise. Life would become quite
impossible if at every turn of events we had to uncover our values
and make out a case for them: why should I go to work or go to
church, pay my bus fare, keep to the left-hand side of the road, be
courteous to colleagues and generally considerate, eat at least one
square meal a day, keep myself reasonably well-informed, offer
hospitality, get a good night's sleep? Sheer practicality requires that
most of the time the reasons go unstated and our values remain
hidden, buried beneath what appear to be instinctive reactions or
habitual ways of behaving.

In the last thirty to forty years 'development' has been one of
those values, generally assumed to be a good thing and especially
good for the poor. By development is meant of course economic
development (though it is interesting to turn up an early edition of *A
Dictionary of Christian Ethics* (SCM, 1967) and discover that such a
meaning does not even occur to the writer of the article on 'development'). In particular, economic development means reproducing in
the Third World or poorer countries the kind of industrial revolution which eventually brought about material progress in countries
like the United Kingdom and has since allowed most of its people to
enjoy higher and higher standards of living. In other countries,

similar developments would be made possible by international aid. The rich would help the poor. They would lend money, encourage capital investment in machinery, power supplies, roads and railways; literally lend a hand by sending personnel; share their skills and technology and management expertise.

Our use of words reveals the value we have come to place on development of this kind. Government departments such as the Overseas Development Administration, research institutions such as the Institute for Development Studies at Sussex University and the Overseas Development Institute, movements such as the World Development Movement aimed at reforming international relations, particularly with regard to aid and trade, are all happy to be identified in these terms. Organizations such as Christian Aid and Oxfam do not complain when described as 'development agencies'. It remains part of the positive image they would like to project. In schools, development education is regarded by many as a desirable part of the curriculum.

'Underdeveloped' on the other hand was soon heard as a negative, not to say disrespectful way of referring to the poor, as unsatisfactory as 'South' (geographically inaccurate) and 'Third World' (plainly derogatory). 'Less developed' sounds marginally better. 'Developing' would be unobjectionable if it did not blur the very distinction between richer and poorer nations which we are trying to define!

THE CHALLENGE TO DEVELOPMENT

But although the value of development has been widely accepted, even assumed, it has not gone unchallenged. Questions have been raised on a number of grounds as to whether it is such a good thing after all. Here are five of them in no particular order of importance.

First, even if it is granted that industrialization, which is in effect what development has meant, brings a greater measure of prosperity, and lifts hungry people well above the breadline, it has not in many other respects led to a better quality of life. Can it be justified unless it does? For example, as people have moved away from rural areas into towns and cities, old established communities, social groups and extended families have been broken up. Instead of having an accepted place in a whole web of relationships making their contribution and enjoying mutual support, the new urban dwellers found themselves in a harsher, unprotective world where they were left to their own devices to win, or more often lose, their way. The mood was competitive rather than co-operative and communal. Work, which continued to make up the greater part of life, became a more narrow and even less satisfying experience for the vast majority. It had never been free from drudgery, but now instead of a rounded existence requiring many skills: growing crops, caring for animals, weaving, hunting, toolmaking and so on; they were restricted to simple repetitive tasks.

Second, on top of the loneliness and the boredom came growing disparities. One was between employer and employed. Those who did the work did not reap the benefits. Expensive machinery, unlike the tools and cattle used to farm the land, or the simple looms used to weave the cloth, was not controlled by the worker. The workers did not choose whether to work or not and on what terms, neither did they own the means of production. They could only offer their labour, which was not always accepted, and when it was and created useful products, they did not get a fair return. They were exploited by owners and middlemen who profited out of all proportion from their endeavours and kept for themselves the earnings which were rightly the workers'. So those with power in the factories and market places grew rich while the vast majority remained poor, often living in conditions as bad as if not worse than those in the countryside.

Third, development has been accused of prejudice. It is generally against the rural areas and in favour of the towns. It was not altogether surprising, of course, that the new industries should be concentrated in the towns, where there were better facilities for production and readier markets for goods, but it only aggravated the steady deterioration of life in the villages. As more and more people moved away in search of work and prosperity, these were drained of their vitality. This in turn fostered the so-called 'urban bias'. In part it refers to a patronizing attitude to traditional ways of doing things from farming to medicine. They were regarded as out of date or primitive. But it also points to increasing discrimination. If the majority live in towns, then towns are regarded as of first importance, and decisions taken by townspeople tend to be made in their favour. The needs of rural areas, for roads, communications, goods and services, agricultural supplies and investment, are neglected and with them their problems including their poverty.

Worse still, the towns were allowed to benefit at the expense of rural communities. Hydro-electric schemes are an oft-quoted example. They entail the construction of huge dams and reservoirs. Forests and farming land have to be cleared. Quite apart from environmental consequences, people are moved and lose their homes and traditional sources of income. Their independence is often threatened as well, as they are forced to work for others on land no longer theirs. And all of this to produce electricity which may contribute to the prosperity of others a long way away but will never brighten their own homes or power their machines. In these and other ways, 'development' and 'urbanization' become dangerously synonymous.

Fourth, development has been criticized as unjust and exploitative on an altogether different scale. When wealthy industrialized nations provide aid in the hope of reproducing themselves in the Third World, it is not actually the poorer countries that benefit, but themselves. Development is a form of investment. The intention is not so much to help a developing nation to stand on its own feet, as to make profits for the investors. To him that hath shall be given. This may make it necessary to create a wealthy elite within the developing country who come to have a vested interest in the successes of the industrial enterprise and are therefore ready to co-operate. It may even require modest increases in wages and spending power to create markets for goods; but for the vast majority there are few rewards or improvements in their way of life. Much of the surplus is transferred out of the country in the form of profits, or interest on government or bankers' loans, or as cheap goods for Western consumers. It is not ploughed back to build up a genuinely independent industrial base within.

Finally, development has been challenged as not only unfair but ineffective. It has simply not resolved the basic problem. The disasters of the 1980s, particularly in the Horn of Africa and Bangladesh, have been enough to bring that home, but, it is claimed, the lesson could have been learnt well before then. The period 1960–70 was dubbed the United Nations Development Decade. Once again, development was assumed to be a 'good thing'. Much was achieved. New industries were created in the Third World, and in many cases they performed well. In terms of output and profits, there was growth and investors could feel satisfied with their returns. But it had to be admitted at the end of the decade that there remained an appalling degree of poverty especially in rural areas: 39 per cent of the population in the Third World was still destitute; 67 per cent was described as severely poor. Whatever benefits had flowed from industrialization had been enjoyed by a comparative few. Few had found work in the factories. Competition and labour saving technology militated against it. Many who left their villages for the 'new world' ended up unemployed or underemployed. The majority continued to work long hours on backbreaking jobs for small returns. If more goods were being manufactured and made available, they did not have the money to buy. Little if anything had changed for them.

In response to these and other questions and criticisms, an alternative to the orthodox view of development arose, smaller in scale, more locally and community based, more participatory in style. It spoke of a counter-culture in contrast to the cloning of Western industrial, metropolitan society in the Third World. It challenged the assumption, if not that development was a good thing, then certainly that industrialization and urbanization on a massive scale were the best ways to go about it. The alternative had a number of persistent features. For many they were exemplified in Schumacher's phrase: 'Small is beautiful': small communities in villages and towns, small property holdings, small-scale industries and production, intermediate technology, small-scale to match our human scale.

For me, the alternative was brought to life on one memorable occasion in West Africa by a group of younger people who had benefited from higher education. They were all set to make it in the city. But they had returned instead to 'rejuvenate', as they called it, the life of their villages where they hoped that many others would soon find equally good reasons to stay. They looked for a reversal of the 'urban bias' in favour of support for rural areas where, they pleaded, farmers should be given the wherewithal: seeds, fertilizers, tools, loans, irrigation and good advice on farming methods, to improve their crops. They worked for new opportunities for women, and organized communities to campaign for new roads and other facilities for marketing their products.

With this concern for the small and the rural often goes a belief in a more equal and equitable distribution of goods and a co-operative rather than a competitive way of life, where land, for example, one of the most important 'means of production', is not owned by a few to exploit the many, but held in common for the good of all. This is not only a more acceptable or human way of doing things, but could be a more effective way of putting an end to poverty. In a small-scale, shared, labour-intensive world, far more people will have work, and therefore money to spend, and that in its turn will stimulate economic growth and prosperity.

Similar emphases find echoes in the priorities of voluntary development agencies and non-government organizations (NGOs). They can often be critical of what they refer to as 'top-down' or 'trickle-down' development, where massive schemes show no signs of benefiting the poor, however confidently they are expected to do so in the long term. These agencies prefer to work instead from the base up, starting with the poorest of the poor, which often means rural communities, and ensuring that as far as possible they are in charge of what is done, that it is a direct response to their needs and that they are the first and not the last to benefit.

The counter-revolutionaries who criticize industrialization and urbanization can themselves be criticized. For example, they can take a somewhat romantic, even nostalgic view of rural life, where women often face a relentless round of toil, cleaning the house, bearing children and caring for them, working in the fields, gathering firewood, laboriously processing and cooking food, fetching water day after day from distant sources, and where a Sunday morning church service can be their only opportunity for rest. The critics can also underestimate the hidden benefits to the Third World of First World investment, and overestimate the degree of exploitation. Many of the drawbacks and horrors of industrial development are not the hallmarks of international exploitation. They have been experienced as much in the First World as the Third. They are the hallmarks of the struggle between labour and capital, employees and employed anywhere in the world; they may not necessarily be permanent where labour becomes organized, and gradually finds its strength; they have even been seen as part of the price to be paid in the short term to achieve widespread future prosperity.

Again, it is probably far too simple to set large and small, city and village, rounded work experience and the division of labour, in opposition; and above all, the industrial and the agricultural. There are limits to the extent to which economic prosperity can be built on agriculture alone. Sooner or later, rising food surpluses will need to be exchanged for other kinds of manufactured goods. And is it always true that industrial and urban development impoverishes the countryside? The sheer poverty of the countryside can drive people towards the towns in search of work and food, whether there is industrialization or not, and urbanization, far from being stimulated by new industries, can move forward at an alarming pace in their absence, engineered as it were by rural deprivation.

DIFFERENT KINDS OF 'GOODS'

My purpose, however, is not to give a comprehensive account of the argument, let alone to settle it, but to point out that throughout this debate, a whole range of value judgements are being made. Not only 'development' but aspects of development are labelled 'good'. Material prosperity is 'good'; technology and mechanization are 'good'; it is 'good' for the rich to help the poor; traditional communities are 'good'; small is 'good'; so is labour, and equality, a co-operative style of working, consumerism, even a degree of sacrifice. In many cases, others are prepared to label much the same things as 'bad' and affirm alternative values such as size, mass production, modernization, every kind of labour-saving device, self-reliance and competition.

To save us from the worst of muddles, it is necessary first of all to make some distinctions. The word 'good' is being used in different ways. Some are of more relevance for us than others. Schumacher's phrase, for example, is interesting: 'Small is beautiful'. In much of what he writes, it takes on a moral tone: small is good for us, rich and poor alike, and we ought to prefer it; but there remains an aesthetic note which refers not to a matter of duty but to a matter of taste. Just as a picture may be 'good' not because it is wholesome and likely to enhance rather than corrupt those who cast eyes on it, but because it pleases me and I happen to like it, so some people may like small-scale communities and enterprises because they are to their taste. Others may disagree, enjoying the big city and the big time; but we can have that disagreement and walk away from it, as from an argument over the merits of a picture, without feeling that too many principles are at stake. This aesthetic use of the word 'good' certainly enters into the value judgements we make. We should recognize it for what it is, acknowledge and tolerate our differences of temperament, but not allow them to absorb too much of our moral energy. Certainly our main business here is not to engage in that kind of aesthetic debate.

The second use of the word 'good' has to do with efficiency. A good machine, like a good system, is good because it works. What is small or big, labour-saving or labour-intensive, co-operative or competitive can be commended for the same reason. It is effective and gets the required results. That claim has been made on both sides of the argument we have been touching on. But it is essentially a technical discussion where moral considerations may be of secondary or no importance, and Christian insights have little if anything to contribute. We shall return to the point in Chapter 3.

Of more immediate interest to us here are the occasions where 'good' is used in the moral sense of being good for people. (By talking in this way, incidentally, I have not wished to exclude the possibility that animals and the material world could make moral claims on us; in other words that we should sometimes consider what is good for them as well.) The small-scale is not simply upheld as something that we like, or as an efficient way of working, but as actually enhancing human life and therefore as something we ought to value and pursue. Even here, however, a further distinction is helpful and that is between what is good in itself and what is good because sooner or later it leads to good results; it is a means to an end. The same value may qualify for both camps.

Take 'co-operation' for example. It may be valued as an acceptable means of achieving the desirable aim of a better standard of living for everyone: 'There is nothing we cannot achieve if only we work together!' But co-operation may equally be valued as good in itself, embodying the kind of mutual helpfulness and friendly relations that are meant to exist between human beings. 'Competition' might prove more difficult to justify as good in itself, but still be valued, along with a degree of inequality, because it motivates people to work hard and it gets results.

What of 'material prosperity'? The First World is both congratulated and castigated for attempting to reproduce the consumer society in the Third World. There is much about it which testifies to the belief that accumulating material possessions is good in itself. When it comes to money, prosperity, cars, household and leisure goods and equipment it seems to proclaim: 'The more the better!'

Those who become prudish and think it ill-advised to encourage the less well-off to follow down the same primrose path, can easily be accused of denying to others what they have long enjoyed for themselves. Sauce for the goose on this occasion is not apparently sauce for the gander. However, there are many additional hesitations about valuing material possessions as good in themselves. The physical world, of which we ourselves are a part, is good and necessary, but it is not enough. We do not live by bread alone. It is the basis and the body for the life of the spirit. It is the possibility and the means for expressing and realizing love and joy and peace and hope and many other virtues. It is more like a means to an end.

So we may value what is intrinsically good and what will sooner or later have good consequences, though we should be wary of achieving those consequences at any price. Having made this distinction, we can perhaps leave it on one side, since either way we are led back to what we value as good for ourselves and good for others, to what is worth upholding and pursuing. We have uncovered a fair number of these values by listening to the way people talk about development. Should we wish to make up our own minds, how once uncovered and even challenged can they be justified?

TESTING OUR VALUES

There are at least four well-known tests. The first has to do with the compatibility of our values with our faith, in this case our Christian faith. In one sense, as we have noted earlier, our values are themselves statements of faith. They will certainly run back to them eventually. We must make sure that the faith we arrive at and confess by that route bears some relation to the faith we otherwise confess as Christians, as it finds expression in the Bible and the beliefs which the Bible and experience have consequently inspired.

Christian teaching is full of statements about God's good intentions for us and the created universe. It is extremely talkative about the will of God and the Kingdom of God and offers many visions of promised lands, desirable cities, new creations, human fulfilment and a new heaven and a new earth as they are intended finally to be. It is important that such affirmations about what is good and our moral values should be all of a piece.

The value of 'labour' is touched on at several points in the development debate. Phrases like 'labour-intensive' and 'labour-saving' suggest a fair measure of disagreement and it may well exist when it comes to discussing the merits of labour-intensive and labour-saving systems and which of them is more likely to help bring about prosperity.

When labour is discussed in its own right, however, all might agree that physical effort, whether we call it manual labour or exercise, is good for us. All might agree that work should be as interesting and satisfying as possible, related to goals we understand and approve of, the most obvious of which is the meeting of human needs. All might disapprove of demeaning and relentless toil or drudgery and seek to remove it. However, Christians will want to ask how all this squares up to the affirmations of their faith. They will recall that, while affirming the physical side to our being and the commonsense need to work, it too believes there are undesirable aspects to human labour: 'in the sweat of your face you shall eat bread'; 'in pain you shall bring forth children'; and that it has been in two minds whether this punishing element can ever be removed. They will recall that it honours a working God, a maker and creator of heaven and earth whose work is not yet done, and who invites others, made like God, to share it. They will also recall that such creativity, by no means confined to artistry, is extremely demanding if the living and suffering of God in Christ is anything to go by. Drudgery is the wrong word for it, but it seems that blood, sweat and toil are certainly needed to build a new earth.

Such a discussion may well be of little interest; it may even be dismissed as idle and insensitive when what is needed for the time being is simply more jobs of almost any sort in a world where far too many have no work and no livelihood. It may be more relevant to test out the value of 'equality', or rather of lessening the disparities between rich and poor which so readily distance and divide us from one another, and ensuring that everyone has an equal opportunity to find their feet and become the sort of people they have it in them to be and that God intends.

Looking at the faith, with its emphasis on love and neighbour-liness, reconciliation and communion, breaking down barriers and making strangers into friends, there would seem to be little room for argument. Christians have nevertheless argued otherwise and regarded a measure of inequality as a so-called 'secondary good'.

If we lived in a perfect world, there could certainly be no argument—but we do not. We live in a world where people do not automatically give of their best or work hard to produce the wealth that could eventually raise everybody's standard of living, unless they see some immediate advantages for themselves. They need incentives. For the well-off, that means the possibility of becoming even better off. For the poor it usually means as few unearned benefits as are necessary to sustain them, so that they are forced to rely on their own productive efforts. So the gap is widened rather than narrowed. Such values seem far removed from the Christian ideal, but they have been defended on the basis of Christian realism. Human beings may be made in God's image, but they are also sinful and self-regarding, and what we value has to take account of both.

A second way of testing out our values is largely common sense. Is anyone else attracted to them? Indeed have these values been upheld by most people for much of the time, or do they represent little more than the idiosyncrasies of the few? Longevity and popularity are of course no guarantee of moral worth. The prophets and champions of justice have often been on their own, and when new patterns of goodness emerge, they are not always readily appreciated. Nevertheless, what is widely respected is not lightly to be set aside, and in any case it is wise to check the company we are keeping.

The merits of metropolis, now as familiar a sight in the Third World as the First, compared with smaller towns and villages, and its ability to offer a better way of life, have long been part of the development debate. For a short time in the 1960s, it seemed as though those who valued the small and the rural had largely lost their case. Radical theologians, most notably Harvey Cox, greeted 'The Secular City' with almost uncritical acclaim. It was not just that some preferred it, or that it had some advantages to offset its apparent drawbacks. It was the way we were meant to live.

The fragmentation of city life, where home, work and leisure were no longer all of a piece, but compartmentalized; the bureaucracy which administered the city's affairs; and the anonymity of vast crowds where most people remained unknown to each other and did not seem to want to know, need not necessarily be seen in a wholly negative light. They were, rather, opportunities and the organizing abilities which made those opportunities possible. Metropolis provided the large and varied arena in which we were finally to be freed from the parochialism and predetermined roles of the village to make our own responsible choices and develop voluntary rather than imposed relationships. It was a paradise with possibilities where we could discover and be ourselves. This revolutionary social change was in line with the Gospel, and the Secular City was a perfectly adequate way of thinking about the Kingdom of God.

Such enthusiasm for the modern city (a very different entity from the smaller biblical city and Greek and mediaeval cities) did not last for long. That does not necessarily mean it was misplaced and this is not the place to draw conclusions. No doubt we should not look back but go on and use our human ingenuity to invent new social arrangements incorporating what we have come to value most about cities, towns and villages; but whatever we value, including a 'bias to the city', it is useful to see who else values it and why, and whether it is a lasting value or not.

Third is what some might call the test of conscience, or what we experience as our instinctive sense of right and wrong—the little voice (of God) within. It is far from instinctive as a matter of fact. It may be part of our nature to be able to appreciate the distinction between right and wrong—we can talk to one another about such matters as we could not talk to the animals[1]—but there is little evidence that we actually label things right and wrong, good and bad according to a 'natural law' written indelibly on our hearts; rather these are attitudes that have been impressed upon us over the years, through childhood, youth and adult life, by family and society to such an extent, that we find it very difficult to think or react otherwise. They are part of the world that has made us what we are and which has formed us so thoroughly that we no longer have much, if any, sense of conforming to it. Its values have become part of ourselves. As such, they are to be taken seriously as part of a moral tradition which may well have persisted because it is genuinely wise; but they are not to be trusted absolutely. They may equally well reflect the self-interest of the social group to which I belong, and reinforce as moral values patterns of behaviour most likely to maintain its advantages over others.

Brought up, like many others, on a long and honourable tradition of 'charity' towards those less fortunate than myself, a value which fits so neatly into the burgeoning awareness of just how much poverty there is in vast areas of the world, and which still supplies much of our moral energy when it comes to development, nothing but a good conscience flows from exercising it. I, along with others, am having to learn however that almost all our talk about rich people helping poor people has to be challenged, not only because it is muddled about who is rich and who is poor, but because of the possessiveness and condescension and unwillingness to act justly which most of it implies.

A fourth and final way of testing our values appears to take us back to the distinction we set aside between 'means' and 'ends' or even to send us round in circles, but it should be mentioned. Unless we believe, as some do, in the kind of divine revelation that announces once and for all what is good, we have to learn what is good from experience. We have to observe as best we can what happens to us when we live according to certain values. The outcome has to be the revelation, revealing their true worth. Or again, unless we believe that our values are 'deontological' which means it is our duty to abide by them whatever the consequences, they are best thought of as 'teleological', promoting a worthwhile end or result and finally to be judged by whether they do so or not. We have to learn as we go.

One tradition in ethics (utilitarian) argues that the ultimate test of a moral value is whether or not it produces the greatest happiness for the greatest number. 'Happiness' is not perhaps quite the right word. It can be a very superficial emotion. To search for other words risks a fruitless exercise which proposes one set of values against which to test another! It remains true, however, that to some extent we have to discover where the best for us lies and watch and wait and see whether what we choose to value and call good, be it modernization or labour-intensive farming, enhances life or diminishes it.

It becomes apparent that if we start out with different, even conflicting values relating to development—the labour-intensive and labour-saving; small and big; metropolitan and rural lifestyle; co-operation and competition, for example—the four tests we have outlined will by no means resolve them. They do not offer us final answers as to what is valuable and what is not. They leave considerable room for variety and disagreement, and that is before we even begin to decide what exactly we are going to uphold (let alone what precisely we are going to do) on any particular occasion when at least two other considerations will have to be taken into account.

One is the need to choose between our values where they conflict or cannot all be respected at the same time. Two such choices have become all too familiar to me. Among development workers, there is in my experience a real conflict between the desire to iron out disparities of income between them, so being true to the egalitarian spirit they would like to foster everywhere, and obtaining in the labour market and at a competitive price the kind of managerial and technical skills and abilities without which their agencies and organizations would be hard put to it to make an efficient and effective contribution to development. Again, such workers can be torn between their own commitment to the poor and their convictions about the best way to bring an end to poverty, and their equally deep commitment to partnerships with the poor and respect for the opinions and priorities of the poor which sometimes they cannot share. Values have to be placed in some sort of pecking order. Moral trade-offs have to be contemplated.

The second consideration is the circumstances within which we have to act, or what in one modern but also ancient tradition in ethics is referred to as the 'situation' or 'context'. What may be good in one place, may be less good or no good in another, and vice versa: what is generally frowned upon may occasionally be acceptable. In Africa I well remember an experienced African development worker clearly committed to rural development arguing long and hard in favour of urban bias. Electrification had to proceed as fast as possible, even though it would mean that the larger centres of population would get the supply while the rural areas got nothing but the disruption and impoverishment which followed hard on the heels of vast hydro-electric schemes. Only such discriminatory measures would ease the enormous demand for fuel in the form of wood and charcoal and de-accelerate the process of deforestation, soil erosion, and desertification. I was in no position to assess his argument, but, sounding as it did like heresy, it did remind me of the 'situationists' who insist that no values are absolute and no action is good in itself; even urban bias, like extra-marital relations (an early *cause célèbre*), can come in from the cold if the circumstances are right!

MAKING UP OUR OWN MINDS

What are we to make of this moral uncertainty, where having carefully checked our values against our faith, tradition, and experience, we are left with ample space for differences of opinion, and where even feeling certain we are right because conscience remains untroubled by no means puts our values beyond dispute? The third of the following three points is to me quite crucial to the argument.

First we should be clear what testing our values does and does not achieve. It will encourage us to question our assumptions, to criticize and reflect. It will add to the stock of ideas in our minds. It will widen the range of moral possibilities. Much will occur to us that had not occurred to us before. It will nourish our thinking. It will indicate where the weight of opinion lies, both past and present, and if we are wise we shall not lightly set that aside.

It will not, however, absolve us from finally making up our own minds unless we believe that there is some superior authority to which we can properly hand over that responsibility. What we gain from looking into our faith, the long and broad traditions of moral convictions, the promptings of our own deepest feelings and our experience of what helps people to flourish, is not moral certainty as to what is good for us or for anyone else, but the raw material out of which we must make a moral judgement. There is an essential ingredient in our values which cannot be handed to us on a plate. We do not create them out of nothing or out of the air. Much is given. Humanity has learnt much and passes it on. But in addition to what is given, there is our own creative contribution. There is the act of personal responsibility which knows it must give reasons for what it values and must respect what others have to say, but must also speak and judge for itself as to what, having considered as carefully as it knows how, it will call 'good'.

Second, and it is implied in the first, if there is no substitute for making our own moral judgements, we should not make them alone. We may have to be responsible, but we are not self-sufficient. We may have to be morally creative, but we are not God. Our knowledge is limited. Our understanding is limited. Our experience is limited. We see the world only from a strictly limited point of view out of one culture, one time and through one pair of eyes. What is good for us and for others is somewhat larger than that, and our limited insights need to be complemented and corrected by the equally limited but different insights of others. If there is then an 'aloneness' about what is good, there is also about it an essential 'togetherness'. We must shoulder our personal moral responsibility, but within the community, a community which includes the poor, we must listen and learn from one another and in many ways that corporate learning process is exactly what the four tests we have spoken of represent.

Third and crucially, if an essential part of being moral is making up our minds about what we value as good for us and good for others, other people must be allowed to make up theirs. We may express our views to them, argue and disagree with them, as, in community, we need them to argue and disagree with us, but we cannot decide for them what their values should be. That is as true of the field of development, and of deciding what is good development and what is not, as it is of anything else. There is a marked tendency in the so-called developed countries to think that we know best, even to look down on other people's values as we tend to look down on their skills and traditional practices (in farming methods and medicine). Nothing may shake our confidence, and we are entitled, as we have said, to argue our case, but their values, including what they value as development, are finally their business and not ours.

At this point we should recognize that an additional value is emerging, and that it is being placed high in the pecking order, maybe not as high as the value of life itself, but fairly high all the same: I greatly value people being left to decide what their own values will be.

Admittedly this value does not always pass the four tests we have outlined with flying colours. If you ask, for example, with regard to the second of them, whether this value has been upheld by most people for most of the time, it is hard to answer 'Yes'. Many, including many churches, seem to have thought it better to tell people what their moral values should be. On the whole, they were not to be trusted to make up their own minds. Again, with regard to the fourth, history has borne witness to the undesirable state of affairs that is thought to arise when everyone 'does what is right in their own eyes'—or does that rather reflect the unease of those whose authority has been affronted? On the other hand, while there is much in my faith which reminds me that we are sinners and are therefore somewhat hampered in our ability to know what is good, there is much if not more which encourages me to think that we are made in the image of God as creative and moral beings who, knowing good and evil, are capable of making moral judgements and fashioning life-enhancing values, and are most true to themselves when they do so.

Good development is not therefore a matter which a First World can settle for a Third World, or the rich for the poor. They need to engage with each other, and should certainly not be left to decide in isolation, but each must nevertheless decide for itself. Here may lie the clue to one of the more difficult conundrums which confront Christians (and indeed members of other faiths) involved in development.

DEVELOPMENT AND MISSION

The article on development in the 1967 edition of the *Dictionary of Christian Ethics*, which made no reference whatsoever to economic development, may well have got it more right than wrong. Surely in talking about 'good development' most of the values we have discussed so far are wholly inadequate. Development is not primarily a matter of raising living standards. It is a matter of human development as the article so clearly assumed. It is a matter of fulfilling God's intentions for us as human beings, and those intentions are spiritual as well as material, if not more so.

If we are seriously discussing what is 'good for the poor' and the responsibilities of rich Christians in a poor world, we shall have to talk about the Gospel and evangelism just as much as about economics; we shall need to nourish people, not just on bread, but on the eucharistic bread of gratitude, and the broken bread of sorrow and redemptive sufferings, and the risen Bread of Life. In organizational terms, if the churches of the First World are to respond adequately to the needs of the Third World, and help men and women to 'grow up' in every sense, then the so-called development agencies, preoccupied as they are with economic and political questions, must work as they rarely do side-by-side and hand-in-glove with the missionary agencies, preoccupied as they are with winning hearts and minds and souls for Christ.

I had a vision of such a partnership when travelling in Zaïre along the great river. I had gone to visit development projects. These small-scale efforts aimed to produce more food through improved agriculture, fish farms, livestock; to provide better health-care; and to call a halt to the relentless destruction of the forest which threatens to make a second Ethiopia in Zaïre. There was much talk as I went about the need for complementary schemes of industrialization, of the scandalous not to say criminal mismanagement of the country's economy and of the debt crisis which is as deep in Zaïre as anywhere in Africa. But as I travelled, I repeatedly came up against another reality. Everywhere I went I heard place-names familiar since childhood; Kimpese, Kinshasa, Bolobo, Yakusu and the like. These were the mission stations (Baptist) from which we had received visitors to our church at home, for which we had prayed and which, along with hospitals and schools, were taking to the poor what was really good for them, namely the Gospel which alone would unlock for them the door to fullness of life. And these mission stations were not just a romantic memory; they were still there! Does not any talk of development fall short unless we interrelate and integrate mission and development in our thought and practice and at the end of the day acknowledge the primacy of the one over the other?

Here we could seize the opportunity to discuss another important element in deciding what is good, namely motive. Christian development workers have often shied away from having anything to do with evangelism in case motives became suspect. They did not want to offer material help in order to win people for the Christian cause—a kind of bribe—and they did not want people to embrace the Christian cause in order to gain access to material benefits—'rice Christians' as they have been called. Some separation of mission and development was called for so that people in need were cared for and seen to be cared for for their own sake, and the faith was received on its own merits. What might have been a good rounded approach was in danger of being corrupted.

But if the motives had been above suspicion, or as sometimes happens, we had recognized they were not and could rarely be so, but preferred nevertheless to have good things done for the wrong reasons rather than not to have them done at all, what is to be said about the claim that development in the limited sense should be firmly linked to evangelism?

Such a view seems entirely right when it insists that economic development is not enough; and if we go on to express hesitations, they should not be interpreted as an indifference to 'spiritual' as against 'material' values, or as a lack of concern that the poor as well as the rich should have every opportunity to flourish and fulfil themselves in every aspect of their being: in body, mind and soul, in bread and circuses, in prayer and poetry, growing up to God as well as towards each other. Again, matters of faith cannot be kept out of the discussion and practice of development, as we have insisted all along. The one with all its implicit and explicit values is rooted in the other, so that if we are to arrive at anything like informed and satis-factory judgements, there is no doubt about the importance of sharing our faith with others along with much else. We need to share what we believe our lives are about, what matters and what counts for little or nothing, what helps and heals and what destroys. We need, as part of the corporate learning process referred to earlier, to open others to our understanding of the Godly reality which sustains us, and redeems us and defines us, just as we need to be open to theirs.

Hesitations arise on two counts. The first is when it is claimed that the faith we share is the final and absolute statement of what is good and beautiful and true. It cannot of course be denied that many, indeed the majority of Christians have believed something of the sort, the faith having been revealed to them directly by God; but it is not the view of all and it would not be mine. The second is when that faith, understandably if it is regarded as absolute, is virtually imposed on people by insisting that this is the faith they must accept and believe either to be saved from a fate worse than death, or, if sal-vation is much the same as health and wholeness, in order to become fully developed as persons.

Such a firm alliance between development and evangelism and such claims for one particular faith seem mistaken, first because they are insensitive to the great variety of faiths, even Christian faiths, which has existed from New Testament times to the present day, and to the way in which that variety simply by being there at all undermines any idea that one of them is absolute. We may be absolutely committed to it, and absolutely convinced of its truth, but with so many other faiths about, it can hardly be the last word.

Second, these claims are insensitive to a related difficulty and that is the equally strong convictions, often bordering on intolerance, held not just by other Christian traditions, but by other faiths outside the Christian family: Muslims, Hindus, Buddhists and more; themselves often families of faiths rather than a single faith, just like Christianity.

It seems more sensible to stop setting absolute and often imperial claims against absolute and often imperial claims to possess the faith which all others must accept to be saved and to be human, and to recognize instead that each of them represents an attempt to understand and come to terms with the Godly reality which sustains us and redeems us and defines us, but an attempt which is inevitably limited as are our moral values. It has been made from a limited perspective, out of a limited experience of God and history, and as such it is not called to rule out all other faiths or to rule over them, but to offer its own insights and receive theirs in a common process of mutual completion and correction and a common search after truth.

Finally, any insistence that good development must in the end involve not just a concern for the human spirit as well as for our material needs, and not just the mutual sharing of the faiths, but also the acceptance of a particular (Christian) faith pays little if any respect to the high value we have placed on moral creative beings creating their own values by making up their own minds in the light of their own understanding and experience, and by taking responsibility for the judgements and commitments they have made. Evangelism must respect the same moral rule as development. It is not for rich missionaries any more than for rich aid and development workers to dictate to the poor.

'Self-reliance' is a familiar term in discussions about development; indeed it is a value frequently and enthusiastically upheld. It is generally thought desirable that people should not be dependent or looked after. Such relationships too easily become occasions for exploitation. If I depend on you, I must largely do your bidding. Even the interdependence which marks all our lives needs our independence as a safeguard. Similarly, the poor who are just as capable as the rich of standing on their own feet, should have the means to fend for themselves. 'Self-reliance' as a concept, however, must be more radical. It must include moral self-reliance where the poor as well as the rich do not have to bow to others but take charge of their own development, not only when it comes to the values associated with its economic dimensions, but in all its intellectual, emotional, aesthetic, and spiritual dimensions as well.

The root question in any discussion of the ethics of development may well be, therefore, whether or not the poor are in any position so to do. Can they decide for themselves? Have they the power to determine their own futures? Do they have the opportunity to choose and take responsibility for their own values? Can they take charge of their development, shaping and plotting its course? If they cannot, but are virtually bound to do and to be what others think best, how do we create conditions which increasingly set them free to go their own way? Should we in fact be discussing development or mission in the poorer countries of our world but, accepting that as their business not ours, focus our attention on the preconditions for both?

– 3 –

Good works

It could be argued that the real debate about poverty and development is not the moralist's business. We know enough about what is good for the poor. Further discussion could be a distraction. The desirable goals, certainly in the short and medium term, are obvious to everyone. What is not so obvious in a complicated world is how you achieve them. That is where the really difficult and urgent questions arise. It is not a matter of what is good but of what will work. We do not need to wrestle with our consciences and argue over our values so much as apply our technical knowledge and skills to good effect. We have a destination; what we desperately need are ways of getting there.

The point can be illustrated at all sorts of levels. We shall look at three.

RURAL FOOD PRODUCTION

First, the level of local rural communities and small farmers where voluntary agencies and non-governmental organizations feel most at home and most confident that they are addressing the problems of the poor. There is no argument here about what our Christian morality or any other morality requires of us. It is beyond dispute that these people, like all people, have the right to eat and drink and rest beneath their own roof. They have the right to be sustained or rather to a sustainable way of life over which they have a reasonable amount of control. For millions it does not exist. In Africa alone in the early 1980s about 70 per cent of the population or 258 million people were unable to meet their basic needs and of those something like 100 million were literally starving.

The most pressing and interesting questions in these circumstances have nothing to do with morality and everything to do with food production. How do you grow more crops and increase your yields? How do you preserve the soil you need to grow the crops, poor in quality and exhausted as it often is, or swept away by wind and rain? How do you safeguard the trees and other vegetation which hold the soil in place and nourish it, and which allow the rains to seep in and water it? How do you break the vicious cycle where drought further reduces the already disappearing vegetation and so creates conditions perpetuating itself? How do you cope with the pestilence that kills by day and night, notably, in Africa, the tsetse fly? It carries a disease potentially fatal to cattle and infests crop growing areas, so forcing the separation of agriculture and livestock and robbing farmers of organic fertilizer and draught animals for ploughing. And how do you prevent the rapid growth of populations from cancelling out all the benefits of an improvement in the supply of food?

For the answers we do not turn to the moralist but to the technician and experienced practitioner (in the Third World as much as in the First) and to thoroughly practical books like Paul Harrison's *The Greening of Africa*. In his book Harrison sets out to tell the stories of success. He reports on tried and tested methods which have enjoyed success not only in one particular region but seem capable of being reproduced and enjoying equal success in many others. He is on the look-out for 'a realistic blueprint'. In other words he tells us what works or is most likely to work.

Some of the techniques are relatively simple and cheap as they need to be if they are to be of much use where resources are so scarce. One, developed in Burkina Faso, amounts to little more than lines of stones. Without them what little rain there is runs away down the gentle slopes of crusted sand. Nothing grows. A water-level made from a hosepipe, costing very little and easy to use, helps to mark out the contours of the land. Shallow trenches are then dug along them and small stone walls, about 20 cm high and 20 cm wide, are built. They stop the water and with it the soil from running away. They hold the water and give it time to infiltrate into the ground. Yield increases are reported to average over 50 per cent.

The techniques of Intercropping and Agroforestry are not all that difficult either. Like the stones they reflect renewed respect for traditional indigenous methods—improving them perhaps but not despising or abandoning them. Intercropping involves growing crops of different heights and depths and growing periods all together rather than only one at a time. Agroforestry, instead of associating trees with fallow ground which has to rest and recover and be cleared before crops can grow again, allows trees and crops to grow simultaneously.

In some cases Agroforestry is known as 'alley-cropping'. Food crops are grown between lines of trees whose roots go deep enough not to compete with the growing crops for water and nourishment. The trees bring many benefits. They help the rains to infiltrate the soil. They protect the ground from too much sun. They reduce erosion and even reverse it. When lopped they provide stakes and poles for fencing and building, and fuel for cooking food. Their leaves can be used to feed livestock and to fertilize the soil. High yields do not come about all at once, but as the quality of the soil improves they are said to be impressive. Harrison gives such methods high praise indeed:

Agroforestry is not only the most promising approach to reafforestation and the supply of fuel, it is also, in yield-boosting forms like windbreaks and alley cropping, the most hopeful avenue for intensifying African agriculture over the next five to ten years, increasing food production and reducing exposure to drought with few or no outside or imported inputs.

Agroforestry is arguably the single most important discipline for the future of sustainable development in Africa. (*The Greening of Africa*, p. 204)

Most disciplines are more complex. Within five years of independence (1980) Zimbabwe's black farmers achieved an astonishing improvement in food production. The government-backed programme which led to it comprised not one but several interlocking measures. Smallholders and not only large-scale white commercial farmers became the focus of attention. Their problems were tackled. Research work addressed their particular needs. High yielding seeds were developed to suit local conditions. Short- and medium-maturing maize varieties were mixed to offer protection against bad rains. Credit facilities were made available to buy the seeds and the fertilizer. Farmers' groups or co-operatives were formed to share out tasks and responsibilities where labour was short. Agricultural-extension workers were on hand to give advice and training. Unlike many in rural areas these farmers were given access to the market. They could sell their crops at decent prices. What is more, manufactured goods and services were available on which they could spend their surplus money once essential needs were met. There was every incentive to do well.

Such success, we are warned, should not be over-drawn. It is hard won and not without its continuing problems. It cannot be reproduced everywhere in every detail. Nevertheless it offers answers to some of the technical questions about food production. In other areas answers are much more difficult to find. Controlling the tsetse fly is one of them. Run-away populations is another.

Efforts to prevent populations growing so rapidly as to make a nonsense of any successful effort to increase food production are not helped by those who advocate birth control and family planning as the simple, obvious solution, any more than the poor are helped by those who regard the whole subject of population growth as the single key to understanding the cause and cure of the Third World's problems. Of course there will be more food to go round if there are fewer mouths to feed, but it could also be said that there will be fewer mouths to feed once there is more food to go round! Cause and effect are not easily separated out. Chicken-and-egg questions abound and progress has to be made on a number of fronts, not one.

High birth-rates are partly related to issues of culture. Large numbers of children can bring pleasure and status and pride. But they are also related to issues of security, overwork and the hazards of sickness and old age. If there are to be fewer children there must be less work for women to do: cultivating, fetching and carrying water and fuel, winnowing and grinding, cooking and cleaning; and so less need for more hands to lighten the load. If there are to be fewer children there must be more rights for women for whom their children, and especially their sons, may be the only access to land and food in widowhood or safety in old age. There must be health care and education otherwise, with high levels or infant mortality, having many children looks like nothing other than common sense. Prosperity will lower birth rates as surely as lower birth rates will contribute to prosperity.

OFFICIAL GOVERNMENT AID

Roger Riddell makes much the same point about the predominance of technical issues over moral issues in his assessment of official government aid in *Foreign Aid Reconsidered*. Not that moral issues are ignored. Christian teaching is referred to briefly and he sets out some of the familiar reasons why the poor have a moral claim on the rest of us. These include the right to life and to what is needed to sustain and fulfil it, and utilitarian arguments about our duty to promote the greatest happiness of the greatest number.

Riddell devotes rather more attention to less familiar arguments about official aid. One insists that the discrepancies between rich and poor are generally justified. The affluent are for the most part entitled to their wealth. They have acquired it justly by their own hard work. They have invested their labour in freely available material resources, leaving plenty for others if they wish to do the same. If it is objected that not everyone gets an equal chance, they see little in the distribution of wealth and poverty to suggest that wealth rides on the back of clear advantages. On the whole people get what they deserve. Some are simply not minded or motivated towards economic achievement. The outcome, though full of disparities, is fair enough and there is no great moral obligation on anyone to intervene. Some have gone further and insisted that there is an obligation not to intervene since any attempt by governments to redistribute wealth by, for example, compulsory taxation, can only be coercive and pose a threat to the moral ideal of freedom.

Needless to say, Riddell is not over impressed by these arguments any more than by arguments which claim that governments have no obligations of any kind, including an obligation to the poor, beyond their own borders. Obligation is based on community, and community, it is argued, exists within nations not between them.[1]

Another moral argument against aid appeals to the duty of governments to act only in the national interest, as indeed they almost always do! That is what they are there for! It could conceivably be in the national interest to relieve poverty elsewhere in the world in order to promote peace and stability and markets for trade; but only on such grounds—that there were real advantages in it for 'us' and not only for 'them'—would a government be justified in giving aid.

Having rehearsed these moral arguments and in general upheld the duty of governments to relieve poverty elsewhere in the world, Riddell devotes by far the greater part of his book to considering not whether official aid is a morally good thing or not but whether it works. The very balance or imbalance of the book epitomizes the point we are making about the relative importance of moral and technical issues. Quite obviously the issues requiring most attention are the technical ones. What is morally desirable is agreed, but how in practice can governments of better-off nations make a difference to the economic well-being of the poorer ones?

The standard 'technique' is to provide aid in the form of capital for investment. In an ideal capitalist world the money would doubtless come from domestic savings ploughing back a proportion of profits into the business. But where there is little or nothing to spare it must come from outside. Along with investment, above all in agriculture and in manufacturing industries, new technology is needed and training in the skills required to handle the machines. From investment will flow economic growth and an economy which in time can stand on its own feet. The benefits will eventually 'trickle down' to the poorest. If there are more factories there will be more jobs. If the country is more prosperous wages will rise and social services like health care and education will improve. If roads are built rural communities will gain access to markets. If more food is produced there will be more food to eat.

A second 'technique' is equally committed to helping the poor but regards foreign aid as an inefficient not to say disastrous way of going about it. The finest mechanism for economic growth is the free market which matches demand with supply and finds ever more ingenious ways of making profits while charging prices which the customer is able and willing to pay. And 'free' means 'free', with free competition and wide open opportunities giving every incentive to personal initiative. Official, government aid is a regrettable interference in this stimulating free play of the market. It stifles initiative, creates a less disciplined monetary climate, and inhibits growth.

Not surprisingly compromises can be found between the two approaches. These recognize that an entirely free market where people have equal chances to make a living or compete with others on equal terms rarely if ever exists. Official aid can address itself to some of the most harmful defects or help to get things going without abandoning its respect for market forces. It can supply a much needed touch on the tiller without taking over the complete running of the ship.

A third 'technique' despairs of all such approaches when it comes to benefiting the poorest in the countries concerned. If foreign investment as a way of stimulating economic growth works, 'trickle-down' theories which believe the new found prosperity will rub off on the poor do not! National income may rise but that of the poor all too easily remains unchanged; and the strategy may fail for any number of reasons. Government corruption is one, though it should not, as it often is, be taken to be universal, or confined to governments in the Third World! Bureaucratic inefficiency and waste may be another. A powerful elite within the country, or trans-national companies based outside may siphon off the profits for themselves. The new-found wealth may never be distributed, and the necessary so-called 'infrastructure', including roads and good administration which would bring the rural poor into the mainstream of the new economic life of the country, may never be developed. If the poorest are to benefit, aid must be targeted more directly towards them. It will only work from the 'bottom' up rather than from the 'top' down through the funding of smaller-scale, local agricultural and manufacturing projects.

We shall need to return later in our discussion to two further answers to the technical question about how you get rid of poverty, rather than the moral question about why you ought to. One is fundamentally suspicious of official government aid, not because it threatens the free market system but because it promotes it and with it the whole Western capitalist system, a system which is not only inappropriate to the very different circumstances of Third World countries and fails in the end to share with the poor any benefits it may bring, but actually breeds by its very nature the inequality and poverty it now presumes to overcome. The only real way forward is to change radically the whole social and political order so that power and influence are in different hands or at least shared out and in more hands.

A fifth 'technique' has less to do with political revolutions than with economic ones. The way to end poverty is not to change social structures but to restructure a nation's economy.

Whatever the technique, whether it be investment, or leaving the market well alone, or channelling resources directly to the least and lowest, or radical social and economic change, if it is advocated as a workable means to a morally desirable end then it invites us to test it out in practice to see whether or not it passes with flying colours. Does it in fact do what it claims it will do? Does it work? Roger Riddell in reconsidering foreign aid tackles that question with considerable firmness and comes up with very few answers. That the vast majority of tests appear to be inconclusive carries implications to which we shall return at the end of this chapter.

Riddell adds an interesting twist to his argument about foreign aid. It serves to underline yet again the greater importance of technical issues compared to moral issues when it comes to deciding what is good for the poor. The argument about what works is not just a technical argument. It is actually part of the moral argument, and on two counts. First he reminds us that more often than not what we do is not morally good or reprehensible in itself. It depends on the outcome. So, 'the moral case for providing aid is only rarely if ever in practice an *a priori* nonconsequentialist imperative; hence it does depend on the effects of the funds inserted'. Second, he suggests that if there is no way in which official government aid can be effective then there is no moral case for governments to answer. We may be obliged to find practical and effective ways of carrying out our moral duty but there is no moral obligation to do what cannot be done. He concludes that several of the necessary steps in the argument 'to conclude that governments have a moral obligation to provide aid to the Third World' have to do with whether or not their interventions will actually work!

INTERNATIONAL DEBTS

The importance of technical issues could well be illustrated further with reference to the environment and disarmament, both of which touch the lives of the poor in immediate ways. On the environment there is growing agreement about our duty to not only sustain the lives of the poorest now but ensure as far as we can that the lives of both poor and rich are sustainable in the future. The more difficult question is how you fashion this intricate and interdependent world for humane purposes without irrevocably damaging it or using up resources like rainforests which may well be both irreplaceable and indispensable.

Debates about disarmament regularly take on a high moral tone: between unilateralists and multilateralists for example; and of course moral issues are at stake. But on many of them we can agree. Destruction on any scale is undesirable, and on the vast scale made possible by modern weaponry it can have little to do with even residual notions of a 'just war'. It is morally unjustifiable. Besides, material and personal resources spent on armaments ought to be devoted to the poor and hungry of the world. What is not agreed is how best to disarm. How do you get rid of weapons without unduly upsetting the checks and balances which are perceived as offering security? How do you increase trust between nations and a sense of living in a reasonably secure world and by so doing make disarmament possible? These are technical not moral problems better pursued with a cool head and without too much moral heat.

We turn however to the international debt crisis for a third and final illustration of the importance of technical issues. The origins of the crisis lie mainly in the rapid rise in the price of oil in 1973. Commercial banks in the United States, Europe and Japan were suddenly awash with huge deposits from the oil producing countries. The money could not be left idle so the banks turned to what they regarded as the more stable countries of the developing world, countries like Brazil, Venezuela, Chile, Nigeria, Zambia and the Philippines, and encouraged them to borrow heavily. Any help by way of loans to the very poorest countries, particularly in Africa, was left to the World Bank and the International Monetary Fund.

Interest rates at first were remarkably low all round and the scene seemed well set to act out a classic case of investment leading to economic growth. That it did not happen was due partly to mismanagement and partly to misuse. Inappropriate and ill-advised schemes were pursued and handled badly. Powerful elites had little interest in an improved economy for their countries—certainly not for the poor—but a great deal of interest in a vastly improved private economy for themselves. They deposited huge sums back in foreign banks and allowed others to do the same. The result was a massive flight instead of an influx of capital. But failure was due largely to the rise in interest rates brought about by the United States in 1980 and 1981 linked as it was to a world recession. Attempts by the richer trading nations to control mounting deficits led to a fall in demand for raw materials such as sugar and cotton, tin and copper, and with it a fall in prices. The developing countries were now faced not with highly advantageous loans on which they could capitalize but mounting debts to repay and shrinking opportunities to earn sufficient money to repay them, unable as they were to sell their products in the markets of the world at decent prices. Many were forced to borrow even more.

Many statistics can be cited to illustrate that what began as a flow of resources from the First World to the Third World ended up as a reverse flow from the Third World to the First. Latin America transferred to the industrialized countries $159 billion more than it received from them between 1981 and 1986. Africa paid $894 million more than it received in 1987. A more human statistic was unearthed by John Clark:

The flow of resources *from* the developing world as a whole *to* developed countries amounted to $25 billion in 1985. This compares with total voluntary aid of $2.8 billion (£2,000 million) from all Western countries. For every pound put in a charity tin, the West's financial institutions take out £9. (*For Richer for Poorer*, Oxfam, 1986, p. 59)

It all began to look like an exceptionally good deal for the richer countries: 'Reverse-Aid' as some have called it. It was certainly not a good deal for the poor.

Once again moral issues abound. Who is morally responsible for what has happened? The governments which borrowed the money in the first place and in some cases misused it? Those which have since taken over, as in the Philippines, and struggled to clear up the mess? The banks which may or may not have been prudent in their lending policies? The United States? Is it right that those who had no responsibility whatsoever, who were never in a position to lend or to borrow because they were too poor and marginalized to do either, should suffer the consequences of what others have done? Should richer nations be winners rather than losers in a situation they created as much as anybody else? And what of the ethics of usury? How much money is it right to make by lending money? Is it acceptable to allow for inflation and the risks involved; to offer some incentive to the money lenders; to require payment for a service which many are all too willing (or forced) to use, as long as it all stops short of outright exploitation?

Given the situation of the late 1980s, however, whatever the moral issues, there could be little argument about what was now morally desirable. The intolerable, crippling burden of debt had to be lifted off the backs of the poor. The pressing question was 'How do you do it?'.

Numerous proposals have been put forward. Debtors could

repudiate their debts, especially those incurred by their predecessors; or simply default on their payments; or give them a low priority ('cap' them) by allocating only a limited percentage of export earnings (10 per cent) to service them. Money lenders could reschedule debt repayments on more generous terms, allowing more time to pay and reducing interest rates. In some cases debts could in effect be 'forgiven'. Government loans could be turned into grants. Banks could be more realistic and make provision out of their profits for loans which will probably never be repaid, in other words regard the loans as losses and be prepared to write them off. Governments could support them by offering tax concessions.

Greater efforts could be made to get rid of the problem of debt at its roots by getting rid of protectionism and trade barriers and stabilizing world commodity prices so that developing countries can earn a living and pay their way (compare what is known as GATT: General Agreement on Tariffs and Trade). Third World countries in turn could benefit from better internal financial management, including management of their debts. Accounting procedures could be more efficient. Unrelated activities of various institutions and government departments could be co-ordinated and monitored. Longer-term strategies for borrowing and repayment could be developed.

Further measures have to do with trading in the actual debts themselves. On the principle that half a loaf is better than none a bank could allow a debtor to buy back the debt at a discount. The bank gets more than it might have done and the debtor pays less overall. Alternatively the debt is 'converted'. According to one proposal (development swaps) it is bought at a discount by a development organization and sold back to the debtor nation which pays for it in local rather than foreign currency. The money is then spent on development projects. According to another proposal (debt–equity swaps) the money is converted into a capital investment in the debtor country in the form of shares in local industry or government bonds: a matter of 'owing' becomes a matter of 'owning'.

Advocates of such proposals have to be extremely careful not to make matters worse. A developing country will want to be regarded as credit worthy in the future and good for business. It will want to attract investment, customers and trading partners. Its reputation will not be helped by too many delays or failures to pay its bills any more than by an over-reliance on the forbearance of others without parallel efforts to puts its own economic house in order. Again, if banks began to make or accept too many financial losses it could precipitate a disastrous loss of confidence. They would no longer attract investors and, as a result, no longer be able to invest or make available the much-needed loans. Some have spoken of a possible breakdown in the banking systems of the world. Overall it is a buoyant rather than a stagnant world economy that promises to do most people the most good, but it will never sit easily alongside endless profitless financial deals however forgivable and forgiving they may be.

PUTTING THE MORALISTS IN THEIR PLACE

A clear understanding of the nature of technical issues—that they have to do with what will work rather than with what is morally good—and of their importance and prevalence in all endeavours on behalf of the poor, tends to put the moralists in their place on a number of counts. First, when it comes to debating what is good for the poor there will be long stretches of the conversation when the moralist has nothing to say. Deciding between one sort of seed and another or between different methods of planting trees and crops or designing schemes to conserve the soil are matters for the scientists and agriculturalists. Finding a way through the maze of proposals concerning the debt and reconciling what seem at times like incompatible goals, is a highly skilled and technical task which belongs to the financiers and economists of this world. The moralist as moralist simply does not know. It is as inappropriate for him or her to comment on what is best as it is to advise the mechanic on how to repair the engine, anxious as all lovers of the moral good may be to get the ambulance on the road and rush the patient to hospital.

Second, if we want to do good we must of course commit ourselves to highly particular courses of action. We cannot rest content with general moral sentiments. We shall at some point, for example, need to argue with our governments whether they should give aid to other governments and at what level and in what form. We shall want to lobby the high street banks about the details of their lending policies. But in taking up any such morally committed position we shall need help. The moralist cannot go it alone. A great deal of wisdom is required which is not derived from faith or values or even the moral experience which is gathered up and distilled into moral rules. Doing what is good, aiming for it and achieving it is a co-operative enterprise. It requires an interdisciplinary approach where ethics, science and technology sit down and work together.

Third, the need to draw on many disciplines and the realization that there is rarely if ever a direct line from faith and values to particular policies and actions, should make us very cautious about insisting that anything is *the* good thing to do rather than *a* good thing to do; even more that it is *the* Christian way to behave rather than *a* Christian way to behave. Our actions should be compatible with our values. They cannot be identical. No moral party or policy, any more than a political party or policy, can claim all the moral high ground. There is nothing in Christian faith or morals as such for example that can adjudicate between opting for the mechanism of the free market or for the alternative of more interventionist policies, interested as we may be in the ideologies behind them. At the very least we must accept that there is moral room to differ.

Fourth, when it comes to doing good, Christians will not hanker after distinctive moral colours of their own. Because they are Christians, it does not mean that their policies and practices will necessarily be different from anybody else's. A Christian aid agency's line on the debt will not necessarily be different from a secular agency's. Different values, should they exist, could lead to the same conclusions, as is the case where some hold that gross disparities of wealth are more or less justified while others believe they should be overcome as soon as possible, and both put their confidence in the free market as the best hope of achieving what is best. The same values can, of course, lead to different conclusions. This logical discontinuity between our moral principles and our moral practices has positive advantages (as we have noted before, pp. 3–5). It gives us the chance to build broader alliances for the sake of the good than would otherwise be the case if Christianity left us with 'no alternative'. The outcome may be a more complicated moral life but it can sometimes be a more promising one.

WHERE THE MORALIST STILL COMES IN

Before the moralist retires from the scene, however, and without—let us hope—engaging in an unnecessary job creation programme, is it entirely true that the larger and more pressing part of the discussion about what is good for the poor is none of the moralist's business?

The 'double-effect'

The importance of weighing the consequences of our actions has already emerged. They alone will answer 'Does it work?' and judge the technical merits of what we do. But they often decide the moral case as well. Ethics are often 'teleological' rather than 'deontological' in character. Actions are morally good because of the 'end' (*telos*) they have in view and set out to achieve rather than right in themselves, or our duty whatever the outcome. There is not much morality in a campaign to persuade governments to rise to the challenge and achieve the UN target of overseas aid budgets that equal 0.7 per cent of Gross National Product (GNP) unless the money set aside will actually improve the living standards of the poor.

But if the morality of an action depends on the consequence, our actions, including the 'technical' actions we have highlighted, regularly turn out to have more than one consequence. In ethics they are regarded more seriously than mere 'side-effects'. They are called 'double-effects' or 'triple-' or more. They can be unforeseen, but once known or imagined (and imagining the consequences of what we do is a vital part of the discipline of making moral decisions) we have to assess their implications for the moral acceptability of what we intend to do just as carefully as those of the main result we are out to achieve. The moralist will therefore be required to express an opinion and frequently help make a difficult choice when one highly desirable effect may be won only at the cost of a second effect which seems wholly unacceptable.

Much of the debate about economic sanctions against South Africa was technical, but it was partly concerned with a 'double-effect' and so became a moral debate. Whatever else apartheid could be accused of, it made people poor and many inside and outside the country believed that sanctions were an effective way to remove it. As new money, or 'hard currency', became increasingly difficult to borrow or to earn in the international community, the white minority regime, pressed by South African business interests and the sheer impossibility of paying its way, would be forced to negotiate an end to the existing social system. But, it was also argued, sanctions would have another indirect consequence. Black people, already earning very little, would lose their jobs if the economy began to shrink. The poor would become even poorer. Such predictions did not go unchallenged: maybe white people and not black people would be affected first and, having more to lose, far more seriously; but if the fears expressed for the poor were well-founded then there was a moral issue as to whether further hardship was an acceptable price for them to pay.

One of the most-quoted examples of a 'double-effect' in debates about aid is that of 'food aid' whereby surplus food from richer nations is transported to poorer nations and either made freely available to people on the edge of starvation or sold relatively cheaply. In emergencies there may be nothing else to do; but cheap and free food does not only feed the hungry. It undermines local efforts. What is the point in a farmer trying to increase food production if no one will buy what he has to sell because his potential customers can buy it more cheaply or get it for nothing elsewhere?

Similarly, a country in the South trying to export its surplus to a neighbouring country cannot compete with a flood of cheap or free offers from the North. Food aid could be a faulty 'technique' which does not work. It could also have morally dubious as well as morally desirable results or 'effects', promoting dependency rather than self-reliance.

The same could be said, as we have noted, of aid in the form of foreign investment. It may well stimulate economic growth. It may also lock poorer countries into an international economic system from which they cannot then escape and within which most of the spoils go to the strong.

The debt crisis confronts us with a major example of the 'double-effect'. It has to do with what is known as 'structuralism' or the policy of 'adjusting' the economies of Third World countries. Having got into an almost terminal economic crisis for whatever reasons, so that a country is forced to borrow more to pay its debt or seek international aid in order to survive, it seems only sensible not to shore up such an ailing economy but to try to turn it round or 'revolutionize' it and make it viable. As a result institutions like banks, governments and the International Monetary Fund agree to help but only on certain conditions. Economic priorities must be revised. Existing resources must be redirected towards production and exports. Imports must be controlled. Spending must be cut back. Belts must be tightened. Credit must be squeezed, and all to a noble end. But as subsidies are removed and food prices rise, and as less and less is spent on education and social services (during the 1980s expenditure on health services fell by 50 per cent and on education by 25 per cent in the thirty-seven poorest countries), who is most likely to suffer? The fact is that it is not only the debt crisis itself but some of the techniques designed to deal with it, including this process of adjustment, which have dire effects on the poorest of the poor.

In the Dominican Republic, women from the area of Barahona had succeeded in virtually eliminating malnutrition when, in 1982, the government accepted IMF regulations. Prices and unemployment rose. Increasing poverty led to a sharp drop in the sales of the farm produce which provided the women with a modest income. Their customers could not afford to buy from them and they in turn could no longer afford to buy the milk that nourished their children.

In 1986 Tanzania saw no alternative but to accept an IMF package which until then it had resisted for fear of the effects on the poor of the spending cuts involved. As a result free schooling was stopped, extra taxes were imposed, the shilling was devalued by 33 per cent, living costs shot up. Subsistence farmers began to sell their cows in order to survive another year. In Butuan in the Agusan region of the southern Philippines women tried to earn a living for themselves and their families by selling home-made rice cakes. Their husbands were unemployed. IMF conditions forced up the price of basic foods including rice, and new taxes made cooking fuel (kerosene) more expensive. The women traders had to borrow money to stay in business. The moneylender charged one peso a day interest on every four pesos borrowed.

These are by no means isolated incidents. The effects of adjustment programmes on the poor are so dire and so pervasive that they have led to the widespread call, originally voiced by the United Nations Children's Fund (UNICEF), for 'Adjustment with a human face': to protect the most vulnerable rather than exacerbating their hunger and poverty. There was every reason for moral concern about technical matters. However good and sensible the primary intention of an economic policy, one of the end results could hardly be said to justify the means.

Self-interested motives

A second re-entry point for the moralist into the larger technical debate about what to do for the best might well be the question of our motives. Here interest shifts away from our rather public statements of what we want to achieve, whether it be viable agricultural programmes, or economic growth, or turning bankrupt countries into countries that can pay their debts, to why we want to achieve it. Is it for the sake of poorer countries and especially the poorest among their own people, or is it for our own sake? The very notion of 'aid', of helping someone else, suggests a measure of generous self-forgetfulness. Almost by definition it is done for the sake of someone else. But it is widely accepted that most aid is self-interested. Governments, for example, grant it in the form of Aid Trade agreements which tie it to the purchase of their own domestic products so boosting their commercial interests and keeping their own people in jobs; they invest abroad in order to profit from new industries or open up new markets to further their economic interests; they use aid to win friends and influence people and promote their own political agendas. Even individuals giving to overseas aid charities are accused from time to time of meeting their own needs as much as anyone else's, indeed of preferring ways of giving, such as sponsoring children in the Third World, which bring them a great deal of personal satisfaction but which may actually do more harm than good in terms of effects they have on poor communities. What we do, and that includes the techniques we have been discussing, may only be morally good if it passes a double test:

it does the right thing for the right reason. Having looked at the consequences, what now of the motives?

I said rather cautiously that motives might well be a point of re-entry for the moralist. Too much concern about them is probably misplaced. Strictly speaking they are irrelevant. A particular method of farming will either produce more food or it will not. Investment will either stimulate growth or it will not. The motives of the agriculturalist or the financier are neither here nor there. Again, being realistic, if we are going to be too scrupulous over motives we are in danger of getting nothing done at all. The world may be full of admirable ways of putting an end to poverty but they are of no consequence without the will to use them and make them work. The best technical solutions will only work if someone actually wants them to work.

In East Africa the rains had failed so often that the flow of water from the land to the sea was no longer sufficient to prevent the sea water flowing in the opposite direction and penetrating large areas of land. No longer washed down and kept free from salt, the soil became infertile. A group of villagers laboured long and hard to create a system of small dams just high enough to keep the salt water at bay. Behind them several thousand hectares of land came back to life. You could tell things were improving by the patches of green grass and weeds beginning to show through. The land was then prepared for planting, but at the crucial moment the seeds were not delivered. An excellent project was in danger of going to waste. The breakdown in this instance could be traced to the inefficiency, not to say the total lack of interest, of government officials who were unwilling to back the local people by supplying the necessary inputs and providing the organization, roads and transport in rural areas needed to do so.

Land can be reclaimed, crops can be grown, economies can be improved, but the key actors need to be motivated. It is unlikely that they will be unless there is something in it for them. Motives at best will be mixed and it is usually preferable to have things done for less than the best of reasons rather than to be over-purist and not have them done at all.

Much of the anxiety about motives takes a rather negative attitude to 'self-interest'. Christians believe they are taught to think of others and not of themselves. The highest form of love is that which cares about the good of the loved one without any thought of benefit or return. It is exemplified in an extremely self-forgetful man who emptied himself and gave away all that he had, including his life. All such talk may be inappropriate when it comes to what can be expected of institutions like transnational corporations, governments and banks. They are not in business to take no thought for themselves. But even where at a more personal level it is appropriate, our talk of self-interest (and it usually is 'talk', sadly lacking in perception and unrelated to how we actually behave) is often over-simplified.

The Gospels for example are not in favour of a total lack of self-regard or self-respect, indeed they often set out to restore it where it has been lost rather than take it away. And self-interest is not wholly ruled out either. If we are to love our neighbour as ourselves, pretty assiduously that is, there is no suggestion that we are not to love ourselves. If we are not to be anxious about tomorrow, that is because there is no need to if we believe in God's care for us, or because it is of little practical use, not because we ought not to. If we are to lose ourselves and our lives 'for my sake' by following in the way of Christ, we are promised that we shall find everything rather than lose everything. If the Jews of the first century are criticized for pursuing what look like self-interested policies which would gain for them the supremacy over Rome and over all their enemies, it is because they are the wrong policies which will not in the end lead to the peace and well-being they so much want: 'Would that even today you knew the things that make for peace!' (Luke 19.42).

Christian teaching about self-interest is rather more subtle and interesting than the blunt statement that it is wrong. It seems clear that we should not pursue our own interests with flagrant disregard for or at the expense of other people's interests, but even that note of caution finally suggests, along with the rest of the teaching, that the real point is not whether self-interest is right or wrong but where our self-interest actually lies: not usually where we think it lies in short-term gains or measures which over-protect us against the rest but where our own good and the good of others coincide.

Considering our motives, then, may well uncover not a moral task but an educational or 'evangelistic' task to put alongside the technical task of discovering what will actually work. It will have less to do with an 'ought' than with an 'is'; less with saying 'you ought not to be motivated by self-interest' than with saying 'this is in your interest and for your good as much as anyone else's'. It will have to convert peoples and nations not to a different set of moral duties but a different set of perceptions. It will understand that people behave according to the reality they believe they are confronted with—enemies or friends, threats or promises. There is little point in trying to bully or nag them into changing their ways unless we have news for them that reality is other than what they thought: that the enemy is in fact a friend and that it is more appropriate therefore to 'love your enemies' than to hate them.

Changing perceptions is not an easy task. The Brandt Report remains an outstanding attempt to take it on. It appealed without apology to the self-interest of the richer nations of the 'North', but it also tried to teach them that their interest lies in fact in working towards a new, more equitable economic order and a more prosperous South. The outcome would be a more stable world community with better prospects of longer-term prosperity all round. The Report fell largely on deaf ears. Any changes or conversions that have come about have had to wait upon the harder lessons of subsequent history.

If we should avoid bothering overmuch about 'motives' their very existence at least warns us against putting technical issues in a completely false, 'amoral' or morally neutral setting. Techniques such as the free market or structural adjustment or investment or agroforestry are not surrounded by some sort of moral *cordon sanitaire*. They are not developed, deployed, exploited or even evaluated by completely disinterested parties but by creatures of flesh and blood including moral flesh and blood. As such they are not merely interested in mechanics. They have their own interests, values and goals—even their technical 'efficiency' is a value which must sometimes be weighed against others. They use their skills and make their decisions as to where and when their solutions should be applied according to their own good reasons. To be reminded that they too have their reasons is to be provoked into asking why they do what they do, and it is a question to ask not necessarily in order to query motives and criticize the developers for self-concern dressed up as generosity, but to understand more about where their activities might lead and uncover the values they do in fact uphold, values which it is certainly the business of the moralist to debate.

ACTING WHEN WE DO NOT KNOW

One of the most striking features of Roger Riddell's painstaking evaluation of foreign aid is that the case either for or against cannot be proved. Many of the technical questions about what will work and what will not work remain unanswered. The evidence, again and again, turns out to be inconclusive. Does official aid, for example, actually increase the savings and investments so crucial for industrial development and economic growth? Does economic growth benefit only an elite within a developing country and foreign investors without, or can it not be accompanied by a redistribution of wealth, or 'trickle down' to benefit the poor? Will a shift to market-based policies have the desired effect and stimulate initiative and competition? Does radical social change, not to mention revolution, offer better prospects for success? Apparently we do not really know.

There are several reasons for our ignorance. Very little evaluation has actually been done, and for understandable reasons. While its importance cannot be overstated, given the dimensions of poverty itself and the extent and variety of efforts to overcome it, evaluation is an enormous and time-consuming task not often seen as a first priority. Where it has been attempted the information on which it is based has been incomplete and not very reliable. It has been gathered in such a way as to make comparisons between one country or programme and another very difficult. The resulting statistics, like so many, are open to diverse interpretations.

Another difficulty is that the goalposts tend to move. Any development programme is bound to extend over a long period of time. It will be later rather than sooner before it is possible even to begin to ask whether there are any signs of success. In the meantime some lessons will have been learnt. Thinking will have moved on. Approaches and objectives will have changed sometimes to such an extent that what we are looking at and trying to evaluate is a different programme altogether. One example, cited by Riddell, is the World Bank's decision in 1973 to target its policies and aid programmes more specifically towards the poor. Good as it was, it did not make evaluation any easier. When the Bank carried out an extensive review in 1985 some of its projects (less than 30 per cent) had been influenced by the change but most of them had not.

In many cases it is difficult to isolate an aid programme to see whether it works. Success or failure depends on so many external factors. A revival of local export industries will be defeated by a world recession or protectionist trade policies. Local agriculture can be encouraged or undermined as we have seen by bureaucracy. Internal government policies can be decisive. War and weather can ruin everything.

Strictly speaking Riddell's point is that we do not have sufficient evidence to say whether official aid works or not. At times however he can sound more pessimistic, and it is interesting to set his comments on rural development alongside Paul Harrison's attempts to pinpoint what makes for success. Both agree there have been successes as well as widespread failures. Both insist that development is a highly complex business. Harrison can paint bright as well as gloomy future scenarios. Riddell speaks soberly of 'considerable ignorance' of how best to promote rural development in the extremely hostile environment of most Third World countries.

Having reached his conclusion that the case as to whether official aid works remains unproven either way, Riddell goes on to use it to retake what he calls 'the middle-ground'. If our present lack of knowledge prevents us from claiming too much and saying that aid is generally effective, equally it does not allow its critics and opponents to say it can never help and that the economic development of the Third World would proceed better and faster without it. We are entitled to argue cautiously in its favour.

For us, interested as we are primarily in moral issues and their relation to technical issues, this cloud of unknowing about what works has two important implications.

First, we should not exaggerate and suggest we know nothing, or go back in any way on the recognition of our need to listen to and learn from many other disciplines when arriving at our moral opinions. We must still respect the technical experts; but their own perplexity, uncertainty and disagreements warn us against respecting them too much. Technical authority, like moral authority, is best not regarded as absolute.

Second, the cloud of unknowing suggests there are limits to the possibility of arguing a moral case on the basis of the consequences of what we are about to do. We must do our utmost to imagine them and calculate them. Where we are ignorant of them we must research and experiment to increase our knowledge. But we cannot be sure of them. We do not always and, in the case of the technical issues that loom so large in the aid debate, we do not often it seems know what works and therefore what the outcome of our actions will be. Teleological ethics are not a practical proposition if you are expected to know the end at the beginning in order to prove that it is morally justified.

What then are we to do, where a large measure of ignorance prevails, to avoid moral paralysis? In the first place, we must accept that much of what we do we do in ignorance. We are rarely if ever in possession of all the relevant information. We do not have the capacity even to collect it. That is no excuse for being more ignorant than we need to be but, to a greater or lesser extent, when we act for our own and another's good, we remain ignorant. The moral logic of that ignorance is not to refuse to act or do our best for people, but to act out of all due modesty fully acknowledging that our actions are inevitably ill-informed. The greatest harm is not necessarily done by those who get it wrong, but by those who do not understand that as human beings we always get it wrong. The response to ignorance is neither paralysis nor dogmatism but standing open to correction and refusing to think more highly of our actions than we ought.

Second, we must give up any attempt to stick the wrong kind of moral labels on detailed policies and practices. It is our moral duty to seek out concrete solutions to problems. They will be in line with our aims as far as we can judge, and compatible with our principles, but they cannot be judged as morally good or bad in themselves, only as workable or unworkable. We shall be paralysed only if we seek to take our moral arguments or justifications too far and invest these solutions with a moral character they cannot have.

Third, at a more general level, when it comes to principles of action rather than detailed practices, there is a kind of 'teleological wisdom' to be had before the event. We do 'know the end' before we start but we must understand the nature and sources of our knowledge. It is not a kind of deontological wisdom despite all events which feels entitled to say: 'This is an intrinsically good thing to do irrespective of any evidence you may care to bring to the contrary'. It is not knowledge laid down or revealed from on high without rhyme or reason. It is not mere theory, untried and untested. It is rather a wisdom born of past experience. Ignorant in many respects of the future and the present, it has learnt something from the past. It is wise after many events and thoughtfully distils its wisdom into moral principles and rules of thumb. We must act with firm commitment but also with caution and with modesty on this *a priori* knowledge in unfamiliar circumstances until, as we expect, fresh evidence requires us to think again. It is to one such *a priori* general principal of moral action that we turn in the following chapter.

– 4 –

Strength for the poor

COUNTING THE HAIRS OF THEIR HEADS

The reality of poverty is so enormous that it is understandable why it is reduced repeatedly to statistics, generalizations and stereotypes. It is difficult to conceive of it, talk about it or handle it in any other way. Nevertheless it is individuals who are poor. Poverty is about highly particular women and men, each of them important and interesting in their own right; and since this chapter comes closer than the others to declaring where, for the time being, my own moral commitments lie, and what I regard as good for the poor, it will be as well to begin by numbering, as it were, the hairs of their heads and recalling who exactly some of them are.

A mother and a father of Ethiopia
We met her by chance on the main street of Mkele, a town in Tigray in the north of Ethiopia. She had walked for a whole day from her village carrying a child on her back and little more than a handful of charcoal. She had made the charcoal from scraps of wood she had been able to collect from a landscape once covered in trees, but now almost bare. She 'sold' it for two handfuls of poor quality grain with which she must feed her child, her blind mother and herself. Her husband had left. She said she would return to the town as soon as she had more charcoal to sell, probably in a week's time.

Much further to the south, the man had two houses, a wife and many children. One house used to bear the marks of modest prosperity. It had metal window frames and a corrugated iron roof. In the famine conditions of the early 1980s, when nothing grew in his fields or most of the fields of Ethiopia, the metal was sold to buy food for his family and schooling for his children. Only the empty shell of the house was now left, open to the sky. They had moved into a more traditional round house, made and re-made from time to time out of coarse vegetation. The man had continued to plant his fields. Two years later the crops were destroyed by locusts. The next year they had had no rain. One planting had come to nothing. When we talked he was preparing to try yet again.

A youth and a mother of Brazil

This 19-year-old youth regards himself as rich, not poor, and his future as secure. He lives in a small area of the forest officially reserved for rubber tappers like himself in Acre, in the far western corner of Brazil. He is rich because he lives life as he wants to, not in the town which he hates, but among the trees. He will tap maybe a hundred trees a day, following his own particular path, deftly scarring the bark until it 'bleeds'. Later he will return to collect the mild white latex caught in a small cup made from the casing of brazil nuts. He spends the evenings at home, in the clearing, eating the same predictable meal, sharing a pipe under the night sky, sleeping in the wooden house on stilts with the animals underneath. Beyond the reserve the forest rapidly disappears.

Her people have also been given a reserve, but almost all of it has already been taken away. As 'indigenous' Indians they possessed the land long before the Europeans came to Brazil, or the Africans they forced to come with them. Now the landowners have driven them off the little they had left. Entirely dispossessed she sits on a hillside overlooking a few hectares of scrub on which nothing will grow. She has perhaps twenty companions: men, women and children. She points to a muddy stream at the bottom of the hill: 'When there are fish', she says, 'we eat'. Halfway down stood a circle of rough wooden crosses. It was where they buried their children. There was insufficient food and no medicine to keep them alive. As she spoke, she nursed a sick child in her arms.

A refugee in Thailand

He was the leader of his community comprising men and women of several different faiths, but all coming from one country. They were Vietnamese refugees living in a camp on the borders of Thailand and Cambodia. There was little to do, fed as they were by relief organizations, except to organize his people, maintain some sort of cultural and religious life, conduct a modest trade with the local Thais and hope against hope that one day he would be resettled. Others had gone, but several countries had already turned him down. He had fought with the United States Army in the Vietnam war, but he had been told he was disqualified for resettlement in the US by an 'accident' of birth. Generations of his people had always moved easily to and fro across the border between Vietnam and Cambodia, his father and mother among them. He had been born on the 'wrong' side. He was not, technically, a Vietnamese.

People of Asia

She was in purdah, dressed in black from head to foot, her face covered by a veil. She had gone to the legal advice centre in a small town in Bangladesh. Maybe someone had obligations towards her. She lifted her veil to talk. She was twenty-three or -four years of age. She had borne nine children, eight of whom were already dead. The one surviving daughter sat by her side. Her husband had divorced her, turning her out of the house. Her parents refused to take her back. Her only income came from occasional work at a local cigarette factory.

They stamped them out hour after hour, lumps of blue plastic were flattened under searing heat. The template marked on them the V-shaped outlines of a dozen straps for flip-flops. The patterned pieces were sent elsewhere in the Calcutta slum to be cut out laboriously with scissors, and then on to the 'factory' where straps and soles were deftly put together by hand and the sandals completed and packed. In one small home, made from wooden poles and corrugated iron, with its low door and dark interior, a family of four had no other paid employment. If they cut at the blue plastic all day they could earn up to 20 rupees between them. On a street corner a woman also worked with her scissors as she managed her 'shop'. She sold potatoes and plums from a dusty slab of concrete. Her husband, a carpenter, had been without work for two weeks. Cutting out the straps supplemented her meagre trading 'profit' of 5 rupees a day. Bed and breakfast in the YMCA hostel cost 250 rupees a night.

Out in the Indian village the tamarind tree had yielded its fruit. The traders, known as the 'exploiters', from markets too far away to reach, came and offered a price. The owner of the tree could not afford to refuse.

Nicaraguan brothers

You could say he had his back to the wall. Behind where he stood with his younger brother, the wall was peppered with bullet holes. Surrounding the houses and farm buildings were the deep dug-out trenches that turned his community into something more like a military outpost. It was high on the green hills of north-west Nicaragua. The Sandinistas made collectives of some of the older estates, but land had also been redistributed and landless people like these two brothers had the first opportunity in their lives and the lives of their fathers to rear their own cattle and plant and harvest their own crops. It was hard, welcome work made all the harder and sometimes impossible by the unwelcome attacks of the Contras. They came with their guns, in the name of Western freedom, to burn and pillage and kill. A third brother had died and their women had been abused in the most recent incidents. Crops and animals had been destroyed.

Two African women

They will never meet, devoted as they are to the same Lord. One swept the floors of a theological seminary in South Africa. Her son was about to be hanged in a Pretoria jail. He was found guilty of murder. He and others had killed a man they regarded as a traitor. He had informed against their people and their freedom movement. What in some circumstances would be regarded as a regrettable but necessary act of war, was in these circumstances condemned as a capital offence. The woman wept for her son and in the evening returned to the separate township with its inferior facilities, where apartheid dictated she must live.

The other woman sat in church in a village in Bas Zaïre, the corridor of land that links Zaïre to the sea. Her normal day began early, before dawn. There were children to rouse and dress and feed and household chores to be done before setting off with other women to the fields to prepare the soil and plant and hoe and water and gather. By mid-afternoon it was time for the long walk to bathe and wash the clothes and fetch the water. Firewood must also be gathered and, carrying an enormous load on her head, she would return home to cook the meal. Before bed there were animals to tend and clothes to sew, maybe for the family or to sell to earn a little extra money. The hour in church on Sunday was the one break in what appeared to be an endless round of toil, a single respite from ceaseless demands.

THE WEAKNESS OF THE POOR

It is tempting to reduce such people to statistics (one of them alone, in South Africa, represents up to 20 million blacks; another, in India, represents 3 to 400 million still classified as poor). It is also tempting to reduce any account of their poverty to an over-simple explanation, whereas its causes, like the people themselves, are many and varied. To go no further than the pictures we have just drawn, when we ask why people suffer as they do we are faced with a wide range of answers. Certainly many have suffered from 'natural disasters' such as drought and 'the years that the locusts have eaten'; but just as significant, if not more so, are the 'man-made disasters' we have, often unwittingly, brought on ourselves. Deforestation which in the end deprives people not only of wood for fuel and buildings, but of soil and rain and livelihood, is an outstanding contemporary example. The sheer number of mouths to feed, the lack of clean water, health care and welfare services, all contribute to poverty. So does war. In almost half the stories we have told it is a prime source of misery.

Where there is no war as such, there is often violence as peasant farmers and campesinos battle for their land. In the economic realm people are poor because they have no paid work to do or, having it, do not receive a just reward. The needy are sold for a pair of shoes (or flip-flops). They manufacture their goods and produce their crops but cannot gain access to markets or trade in the markets on fair and equal terms. This is true at both the local and the international level and at both the poor can be exploited and plunged into debt. Beyond the economic order are social and religious customs which consign a woman to drudgery or leave her without husband, house or home; and beyond that lies the power of ideologies such as 'Western freedom' and 'Marxism' and 'apartheid' to grind the poor into the dust. And it is not only a matter of the number and range of causes but, as we have noted in the case of rising population levels, their inter-relatedness. The threat to the rainforests of the Amazon, for example, is a meeting place of environmental issues, the debt crisis, unemployment, struggles over the land and human rights, internal government policies, and the oft-questioned activities of transnationals, all compounding one another in a complex tangle of cause and effect.

Such complexity suggests the need to work patiently on several fronts at the same time, trying as best we can to understand and respect the connections between them. To advance any single cause or cure does not face up to the reality of poverty or to our moral duty, but actually evades them both. No such evasion is intended here, and if we now pursue one particular issue it should not be taken as excluding all the rest.

Careful observation suggests that the poor often share a second common characteristic besides the obvious one of their material deprivation. It might be called their 'weakness'. It is not an intellectual weakness which cannot comprehend the difficulties or find a way through; it is not a spiritual weakness which lacks the power to resist and endure; and it is not a weakness of character which lacks initiative and determination, though doubtless the poor have their fair share of such weaknesses along with the rich. This 'weakness' relates to the lack of opportunity to decide or control what happens to them. Others decide about them. Too often they are objects not subjects; and it is this 'weakness' which provides the clue not to the whole, but a highly significant part of our moral duty towards them.

The woman of Mkele did not decide to devastate the landscape or go to war. Her distant neighbour in the south did not decide that his only source of income would be to sell his house. The young rubber tapper did not decide to sell off the forest and threaten his own future. The indigenous Indian mother did not decide to retreat to the most barren piece of land within her reservation. The refugee did not choose to flee his country or be excluded from another. The woman in Bangladesh did not decide to live on the street. The Indians in the slum did not fix their low wages and those in the village did not decide to sell their crops at give-away prices. The Nicaraguan did not decide to carry a sword as well as a ploughshare and fight his enemies rather than farm his land and feed his family. A woman does not decide on hard labour for most hours of the day and night. The Blacks in South Africa did not decide to be forcibly removed from their homes and farms or to be incorporated into Bantustans.

Of course people are capable of contributing in their own small ways to their own misery, and of course there are the forces of circumstance, but for the most part it is others who decide about the poor. It is governments at home and abroad who decide, big business, transnationals, banks, alliances of nations, often the First World rather than the Third, landowners and landlords, middlemen, minority regimes, elites, men rather than women; and they almost always decide in favour of what they regard as their own best interests or the interests of those they most obviously represent, rather than the interests of the poor. It is in this imbalance of strength and weakness, of the opportunity to decide and the lack of it, that lies the endless occasion for adverse decisions against the poor and the perpetuation of injustice and misery. The strong have the advantage and they take it. Where lies the remedy?

REDRESSING THE IMBALANCE

When in the previous chapter we looked at some of the 'techniques' or means of putting an end to poverty, such as official aid and structural adjustment policies, we noted that in some circles there was little confidence in such economic measures unless accompanied by social and political changes, not to mention revolution. What was needed was 'structural adjustment' of a different kind, which re-ordered society in a completely different way. Attempts to adjust the imbalance of strength and weakness might be seen in this category. What is not being contemplated here, however, is a simple reversal of the situation so that a new imbalance is created where those who were once weak are now strong and the strong, weak. That would be to fall foul of a romanticism about the poor which helps no one, and the false assumption that if only another set of human beings were in charge and could have their way, things would necessarily improve.

We are certainly to regard others as made like us in the image of God, equally created and equally capable of taking wise decisions about their lives and ours; and we must certainly avoid the unfounded prejudice that if others get the upper hand things can only be worse. But they, like us, are also limited in their outlook and understanding and prone to make mistakes. More seriously they, like us, are perverse, motivated by unenlightened self-interest and just as likely to make decisions which narrowly favour themselves and are detrimental to others once they are in a strong enough position to do so. If the rich are not to be wholly written off as not to be trusted and entirely responsible for the unjust ways of the world, the poor are not to be credited with total innocence and everything that is to be admired. Rich and poor are equally capable and culpable and both will oppress and exploit other people given the opportunity.

The remedy, therefore, for the imbalance which breeds injustice is not to reverse it, but to redress it, replacing it with something nearer to a balance of equal strength. No single move will bring that about, but of every move we contemplate it should be asked whether it might contribute to this better balance rather than continue or exacerbate the imbalance of the status quo.

Out of three possible strategies for creating a balance of strength we shall concentrate here mainly on the third. They are not, however, to be thought of as alternatives but as complementary. All three of them need to be pursued.

Appealing to the strong

The first appeals to the better nature of the strong and to their enlightened self-interest; it intercedes with them by way of well-informed and persistent campaigns and lobbying in the hope that they will give up some of their power. They will decrease so that the poor and the weak may increase. Obvious examples would be: in the political realm, moves towards fully representative and democratic forms of government; in the economic realm, fewer protectionist measures by First World countries and such groupings as the European Community, and more favourable, not to say fairer, terms of trade for the Third World; in the world of agriculture, redistribution of the land; in the business world, more control over transnational companies for the countries in which they operate; with regard to the debt crisis, 'forgiveness' and with it a loosening of the hold of the First World on the Third; in the military sphere, disarmament.

There are serious problems about all such 'obvious examples'. The problems should never become excuses for not working hard and long to bring them about, but they should modify our expectations. One problem is their complexity, especially in the economic realm. Even with the most iron will in the world it proves difficult to control an economy so that desired goals are achieved, or to bring about a new economic order which is both prosperous and equitable. Another problem is that appeal as we might and as we ought to the strong, history gives us little ground for confidence that they are likely to heed the appeal and voluntarily hand over their power. Yet another problem is that the wheels of history grind slowly. These shifts in power have the potential to affect far more lives for good than, say, any more locally based, community development work could ever hope to do, but they take a long time to come about, should they be allowed to come about at all. The remoteness of achievement can seem ill-matched to the immediacy of the sufferings of the poor which they are intended eventually to remove.

Solidarity with the weak

A second strategy for creating a better balance of strength adds the strength of the more powerful to the struggles of the weak. It lends its strength rather than handing it over. It stands with them and by them in acts of solidarity. It takes on some of their partiality. It takes sides rather than, in detachment, trying to be fair to all sides. It raises their voice and advances their point of view even where it is not exactly its own, not least where that voice and that view will otherwise not be heard.

Throughout much of the 1980s officialdom in North America and in Britain had scarcely a good word to say for the Sandinistas of Nicaragua. Dismissed as an undemocratic, communist threat to freedom, their genuine efforts on behalf of the poor of their land went largely unsung and certainly unaided. Again, the voice of the poor Palestinians of the West Bank and the Gaza Strip was scarcely heard during the early stages of the *intifada* or 'uprising' and all that went before it. To stand with such people, as many solidarity groups in Europe and the United States have tried to do, and speak up for them and find ways of allowing them to make their case is not to put them entirely beyond criticism; but it is to take sides where all too many are on the other side, and to add strength to the justice of their cause.

Strengthening the poor

A third strategy is to work in ways which increasingly free the weak

71

from having to rely on the goodwill of the more powerful or their readiness to share power, adding to their strength until they can stand their ground and claim what is theirs, not because of the beneficence of others, but by right. Here the strong are not asked to give up their strength, it is taken from them in the sense that they are gradually confronted by a growing strength which begins to match their own and erodes it, and prevents it from having all its own way.

There are those in today's world who believe that one way to strengthen the poor, in Southern Africa or Central America for example, is to supply them with arms. The reasons are often cynical, since the suppliers will profit greatly from the arms trade, but not always or completely so. This is not the place to enter the debate about the moral rights and wrongs of armed resistance, only to register respect for five positions.

The first is the pacifist which, on its understanding of the nature and requirements of Christian love, holds that all such activities are ruled out absolutely. The second is the more pragmatic view which judges them to be unproductive and worse: violence breeding only more violence and solving nothing. The third, popular enough among Christians in Europe in the first half of this century, still feels able to make sense of arguments about 'just wars' and 'just revolutions' despite the enormous destructive power of modern weaponry, and to conceive of armed resistance as the lesser of two evils. The fourth recognizes that in circumstances where the weak are already violated and have no peaceful way of resisting, there is very little choice and that debates about the moral rights and wrongs of taking up arms are a luxury denied to them. The fifth position, while maybe disagreeing with the decision and believing that armed resistance is not the way forward, nevertheless upholds the right of those most immediately affected to make their own choices.

There are, however, many other ways of adding to the strength of the poor besides supplying them with arms, and considerable if insufficient resources of skill and energy and money channelled through voluntary and non-governmental organizations and churches are available to pursue them. Most if not all of them will tend to work from the 'bottom up' rather than the 'top down' taking as their starting point the strengthening of local communities in their immediate struggles. One such way is to enable the weak to exploit the law as it stands on land, for example, or human rights and to defend themselves and prosecute their cause as effectively and persistently as the more powerful are able to prosecute theirs.

Another is education so that the weak become better informed and more understanding about their circumstances and how they have come about and are now perpetuated, so that 'knowing the score' they are better placed to make moves to their own advantage. A measure of financial independence for an individual or a community adds to its strength; so does an agricultural scheme which comes as close as it can to being self-sufficient and 'inward-looking' in the sense that it relies very little on inputs such as farming equipment, inappropriate technology, seeds and fertilizers which have to be supplied from outside.

One of the most important ways of adding strength is by organizing often highly individualistic people who have learnt from bitter experience to trust no one so that they find their strength in one another. But it may be as well to give one or two concrete examples which can be related fairly directly to the pictures of particular people and places we drew at the beginning.

In Bangladesh a group of peasant women form a small co-operative. By appealing to the law on land rights and with a modest amount of financial help, they are able to buy a plot roughly the size of a football pitch and have it dug out and turned into a deep tank. The tank is filled with water and stocked with fish. It is surrounded on its banks with banana trees. The fish pond has been overwhelmed twice in recent years by floods in which most of the fish were lost; but the women persisted. When all went well they were able to feed their families on a more nutritious diet, but were also able to sell surplus products on the market. The result was a modest profit and a 'co-operative' bank balance held jointly by the women as a shared community fund.

Besides their improved health and the agreement to work together and so achieve what none of them could have achieved alone, it was this fund which was a principal source of added strength. Previously, when money was needed in a family crisis when, for example, extra food or medicines were required for a sick child, there was no choice but to borrow from the moneylender who rapidly became the debt collector, forcing people to sell possessions including land to pay off their debts or alternatively to borrow even more. He was the strong man with considerable power over the weak. Now the shared money in the bank, made available when needed as an interest-free loan or grant, offered protection from the predators and the prospect of financial independence and freedom from their clutches.

In the same village informal adult literacy classes were being run along lines advocated by Paulo Freire.[1] Men and women were not just taught to read and write, though that itself made it less easy for others to take advantage. Nor, under the guise of education, were they filled with information which was of little immediate use in their struggle against deprivation. Key words and concepts from daily life were not only learnt, but discussed. 'Land' clearly had to be one of them and as they learnt together to read it and write it, they also asked about who had land (a few) and who was landless (the vast majority) and why this was so and what difference owning land made to a family's life. These discussions led to a growing awareness or consciousness of the power and relative prosperity that went with land and of the process, often unjust and exploitative, by which it was accumulated. The gross disparities began to be seen in a different light. They were not simply 'the way things are' and were not perhaps beyond challenging and changing. A weak fatalism which saw no possibilities began turning, through analysis and understanding or 'education', to resolve.

In Senegal a newly developed mango grafted on to the old like a rose on to briar promised greater strength for the small producer in the market place. In many situations his prospects can be improved by removing the middleman. Better roads, or transport shared on a co-operative basis, can give producers direct access to the market. In this instance the middleman remained, but no longer entirely on his own terms. The traditional mango, once ripe, had to be sold immediately or the crop would go bad and be lost. The first and only offer made by the middleman, and fairly low as it was, could not be turned down. The new variety once ready could be left and would not deteriorate for up to six months. That by no means resolved all the marketing problems, but it did give the producer more bargaining power. He was at least open to other offers, and could wait a while until market conditions were more favourable.

In Madhya Pradesh in India a whole community had been forced by growing debts into bonded labour. Having sold their possessions in an effort to repay, they had finally to sell themselves and their children to overlords who, in return for their labour, provided no more than the minimum required to keep them alive, and then not in money but in kind. An appeal to the courts on the basis of existing law secured their freedom. Such freedom, however, was worth nothing if there remained no alternative source of income and no escape from a renewed cycle of deprivation and indebtedness. Freedom had to be followed by job opportunities. Market research looked at a range of goods and services, and wherever a demand was indentified, women and men were trained at a local polytechnic to meet it. As a result many of the bonded labourers were no longer entirely at the mercy of others for a livelihood. Instead they became self-employed shopkeepers, weavers, carpenters and small farmers. Some repaired bicycles or hired them out.

In South Africa the importance of organizing in the struggle against apartheid, and of re-organizing again and again after networks such as street committees and civic associations in the townships, and crisis committees in the mushrooming squatter camps, had been destroyed and leaders removed, was never in doubt.

In Brazil the rainforest is being cut down to earn hard currency for the government and make profits for foreign investors and create jobs for some of Brazil's own unemployed. It poses a direct threat to the environment and to the capacity of the land to grow anything at all in the future. For a while cattle can be fed on the newly created 'pasture lands', but within a few years the soil is exhausted and fertilizing it is uneconomic. Not even the forest will grow again. The destruction of the forest also threatens the livelihood of the rubber tappers. Like many others they have formed co-operatives to give them more weight in the markets, but, of more importance, they have formed themselves into workers' unions to resist the destruction of their way of life. Together they have drawn the attention of the international community to their plight. Together they have physically resisted the bulldozers by sitting down in front of them. Together they have challenged the predatory landowners and their hired gunmen in the courts. Together they have protested and won some concessions from the government, such as reserved areas of the forest which are to be protected from so-called developers and in which the rubber tappers can continue to work and live. Their strength, however limited, is in marked contrast to the scattered and unco-ordinated groups of indigenous Indians in the same country virtually wiped out as communities and seemingly unable to defend themselves at all.

THE MORALITY OF A BALANCE OF STRENGTH

I have explained and illustrated a general approach which sets out in different ways to redress rather than reverse the imbalance of strength and weakness which so often characterizes the disparity between material wealth and deprivation, the rich and the poor. It remains to relate such an approach to our previous discussions about the insights of the Gospel (in Chapter 1), our values (in Chapter 2), the technical ways and means of achieving desired ends (in Chapter 3), and other aspects of the moral debate about what is good for the poor.

To begin where the previous chapter ended, it is not hard to see that in working for a balance of strength we are applying a general principle which may contribute to justice, but does not of itself yield any highly particular proposals for adding to the strength of the poor or overcoming poverty. Indeed we could not claim that such proposals and possibilities are always easy to see. It does, however, provide one important guideline against which any particular proposals may be tested. It is not a substitute or any escape from the search for technical solutions, but it does drive us towards them and give ground for approving of them when they work. We shall want to know not only whether they produce the goods such as more food and water and health and education, but whether they leave the poor with, say, a firmer grasp on a local economy or better able to stand up by themselves and for themselves than when they started.

Again it is not difficult to appreciate the *a priori* nature of this general principle at its own level. At the highly particular, technical level it cannot predict what will work. It cannot tell us whether a small business is viable and will lead to self-sufficiency, or whether an educational method will increase understanding. At another level it can predict. It knows the end of the affair at the beginning and that is because it is the child of enormous practical experience. In the past it has been confirmed over and over again that where strength is matched with strength and not allowed to overwhelm weakness, it is less likely that the worst of injustice will be done. As a result we can now be wise before the event.

What may be far more difficult to accept is that this general principle is of a very high moral order, for is it not manifestly sub-Christian, both with regard to the means it adopts and the end it sets out to achieve?

A SUB-CHRISTIAN MEANS TO AN END

First, the means which, though one of considerable importance, is not, as we have repeatedly stressed, the only means by a long way of achieving what is good for the poor, does not draw very deeply at all on the insights of Christian faith. As a matter of fact, Christian faith has quite a lot to say about workable techniques and how you effectively move from the undesirable situations in which we find ourselves to where we ought to be and where most people would far rather be. Christianity talks about redemption, and the coming of God's Kingdom and the making of a new heaven and a new earth. They are all ways of looking forward to a state of affairs which is preferable to the one we now experience, where all that is wrong will be put right and all that remains sadly unfulfilled about our life together with other human beings and with God will blossom and flourish. Pictured in terms of poverty it will spell the end of it, for 'they shall hunger and thirst no more' and the famines of the world as we know it will be turned into something more like a banquet or feast in God's Kingdom.

But if Christianity constantly talks as if there is somewhere to go, it talks at equal length and with great seriousness about how it is possible to get there and how such a new world can be achieved. It offers its own 'technical' solutions. It has views as to what will work and what will not. They are thought to be exemplified in the teaching and living of Jesus of Nazareth who, when dealing with those who in his judgement do not know the way that leads to their peace, implies that he has more promising lines of action to offer them: lines which, ironically enough, are open to the 'poor' and the 'weak' rather than closed to them!

One way of achieving the desired end is the way of prayer: these things come about by prayer and fasting. It probably has much to do with believing that God is already hard at work for good within the fabric of the world's life; trying in the light of all we know of God in Christ to discern the divine way of working and, having contemplated it, then aligning ourselves with it rather than going against it as we so often do; willing what God wills, so drawing on and adding to the divine energies for good.

Two of the major characteristics of what Christianity would regard as promising means to the desired end or the divine way of working, are encapsulated in the words 'sacrifice' and 'forgiveness'. We can hardly do either of them justice here, but 'forgiveness' involves an extraordinarily inclusive way of treating people despite any assessment of them. That assessment may at times be wrong. People can be dismissed and marginalized as 'sinners', as some apparently were in the time of Jesus and the poor frequently are today, when what has happened to them is hardly their fault at all. The assessment may not, on the other hand, be far off the mark; nevertheless while 'forgiveness' remains clear-eyed about moral characters, it accepts even bad characters as potential colleagues and companions rather than shut them out as jeopardizing any common enterprise for good which may be afoot. Forgiveness loves its enemies by refusing to act as if the most hopeful way forward is to keep them firmly at a distance and out of harm's way, assuming instead that they can, despite their reputation, make a constructive contribution. It puts trust in people who do not inspire it.

'Sacrifice' points to a certain readiness to be vulnerable rather than play safe. It is unprotective of the self, prepared to 'lose it' or put it at risk. It gives the self away rather than hiding it or 'saving' it up. It is extraordinarily generous not just in its treatment of others, but in its expenditure of its own resources. It knows well that if anything is to be resolved or renewed then something and someone has to give. It is the close bosom friend of forgiveness in that rather than being defensive it allows others in on relationships where they can either seize the creative opportunity such openness provides or betray trust and do much harm. It is more than likely to be aware of the considerable personal expense involved—of the need for fasting—in moving the world on effectively towards the Kingdom. The Christian story is rather adamant that sacrifice will almost inevitably lead to crucifixion and that only when we are ready to go to such lengths will the end be achieved.

On these two counts alone the principle of achieving a balance of strength as a way of achieving the good is sub-Christian: neither 'forgiveness' nor 'sacrifice' plays any part in it whatsoever. On the contrary it appears to embrace their opposites. Enemies remain enemies to be treated with the utmost caution. No one trusts anyone else or takes them into their confidence. There is not the slightest hint of what is sometimes referred to these days as 'the politics of forgiveness' rather than the politics of conventional notions of power; and nothing is risked or given away, everything is very carefully protected.

Strengthening the poor as a means of overcoming poverty is also sub-Christian in its low estimate of the people involved and their likely behaviour, indeed that low estimate appears to be its main inspiration. The Christian faith and its analysis of human nature certainly recognizes our limitations and perversity: we are 'mortal' and we are 'sinful'. But equally it recognizes our potential as made 'in the image of God'. We are capable of mirroring a more divine way of behaving. We can, like God, make creative moves in unpromising situations. We can, like God, be imaginative and inspired and lift ourselves out of the rut. We can enter, as God has entered, the unattractive situation of another, sit where they sit and empathize. We are able to love and put our immediate interests in second place from time to time. We can 'forgive' and give others another chance despite their record. We can be generous to the point of sacrifice. But no one would ever think that any of this had been taken into account by those who advocate a policy like achieving a balance of strength. It is for dull and stubborn creatures who can get little further than sizing up each other and then locking in battle.

Two remarks can be made at this stage by way of reply. The first is that while it is true that 'adding to the strength of the poor' takes very seriously indeed the more sombre aspects of human nature, it has not ruled out all opportunities for other, more welcome aspects of our nature to find expression. It has not been advocated here as the only strategy to be deployed. On the contrary, we have said quite explicitly and more than once that while it is indispensable, it will not do by itself. Mention has been made of inviting the strong to forgo some of their strength for the sake of the weak and the poor.

That is an invitation to a measure of trust and vulnerability. Mention has been made of cancelling debts or turning loans into grants and gifts. That is misleadingly thought of as an invitation to 'forgiveness' unless it is all-round forgiveness which acknowledges the moneylenders' mistakes along with the debtors'; but it is certainly an invitation to generosity. Mention has been made of improved international trading agreements and enlightened aid programmes. However true it is that in the long run they will be in everybody's best interests, initially they will be experienced as invitations to the rich to exercise restraint or even to sacrifice some of their advantages.

GROUPS AND INDIVIDUALS

Second, however, while there are plenty of opportunities for generosity, it is not just a rather sombre Christian analysis of human nature which breeds scepticism as to whether that generosity will often or ever be shown. There is also the fact that, for the most part, these invitations are issued to groups and social classes and large institutions including companies or banks, governments and alliances of nations. We are not talking about individuals; and it is much more difficult for such corporate bodies to take the better part than it is for individuals, and much less likely that they will do so. It cannot be entirely ruled out. They could just possibly act with the kind of 'forgiveness' and 'self-sacrifice' we have described since even large groups are made up of individuals and led by individuals and develop a certain *esprit de corps* which can be good as well as bad. But it is unlikely.

It is still more difficult to imagine them acting with the sensitivity and delicacy and risk that activities like forgiveness imply. For one thing, corporate decision making, management and control have to be exercised in highly impersonal and formal ways and those responsible are often obscure and remote. For another, people tend to behave less well in large social groups than in small groups or as individuals,[2] not least because the very reason they got together in the first place was to defend themselves and their immediate interests over against those they regarded as their competitors or rivals or potential or real enemies. They were not created for the benefit of those who did not belong!

Large corporate institutions, when it comes to scale, can do infinitely more than individuals to transform the lives of the poor, but they do not have the same capacity for generosity and love. Individuals cannot act on anything like the same scale but, while there are no guarantees, they are capable of Christ-like 'forgiveness' and 'sacrifice' with all their divine potential for good. The results may be difficult to calculate, but according to the Gospel they may also be immeasurable, rubbed like salt into the wounds of the world saving it from the worst; hidden like treasure which is worth selling everything else to buy; apparently dead and buried like seed from which the great tree of the Kingdom mysteriously takes root and grows.

Four arbitrarily chosen examples must suffice to represent this incalculable range of redemptive activity. In the Amazon rainforest Chico Mendes emerged as the leader of the rubber tappers and their workers' organizations in the mid-1980s. He knew very well that any leader who seriously challenged the powerful vested interests which threatened his people stood to lose his own life. That did not deter him. In December 1988 he was killed by hired gunmen outside the small back kitchen of his wooden house where he lived with his wife and family.

In the huge slums of the city women are forced into prostitution to feed their children. Exploited and humiliated, they are finally cast out. One such prostitute is appointed to the staff of a small local development group, working with the poor and the marginalized. They seem to have some understanding of the divine forgiveness, since there is about the appointment none of the sticky, patronizing attitude which forgives sins which either do not exist or merit as much or as little moral stricture as everybody else's, and a great deal of the ability to accept those who have been written off and welcome their contribution. That woman has done much to unionize the prostitutes who now provide facilities for their children, and enjoy improved health care and marginally better working conditions.

In South Africa countless heroes and heroines have worked tirelessly to end apartheid and all the poverty and oppression that goes with it. Many have been to prison where they have been ruthlessly interrogated and tortured. There are inspiring reports about their loyalty to their own kind, and their refusal to inform, often costing them dear. There are also curious reports about their attitudes to their captors, with references to turning the other cheek, loving their enemies, forgiving those who do them wrong. One has spoken in terms of the parable of the sheep and the goats and the duty of Christ's people to the least of Christ's brethren and of how he saw the 'least' in these his persecutors rather than in himself, more destitute than the hungry and thirsty since they had lost even their own humanity. It was to their needs, the poorest of the poor, that he, out of his own poverty, felt called to respond.

In England an old-age pensioner sends a money order for almost

£2,000 to a voluntary agency working with the poor of the world. Her husband had been injured in an accident. They had received compensation. It might have given them respite from being endlessly hard-up, but she saw no reason to keep it for themselves when others had even less. She gave out of her poverty almost all that she had.

VOLUNTARY AGENCIES

Voluntary aid and development agencies in the First World, including those sponsored by the churches, and voluntary groups and non-governmental organizations in the Third World, including again the churches, can provide an interesting and important link between comparatively wealthy individuals and attempts to strengthen the poor. As members of nations, shareholders and customers of businesses and banking enterprises, members of social classes, these individuals would hardly look kindly on strategies which aimed to erode their own power. As individuals, however, we have argued, they are capable of rising above the group mind which is set no higher than its own immediate self-interest, and lending these strategies their generous and quite often sacrificial support. The most obvious way of doing so is by sharing with the poor substantial amounts of money transferred by agencies to partner organizations overseas and used by them to fund educational programmes, co-operatives, agricultural and income-generating projects, legal aid programmes, unions and people's organizations which may well look forward to a time when they can stand on their own feet and announce that 'we have now no need of you', but which in the initial stages of their development depend a good deal on outside resources.

Where such hopeful alliances are formed between those who might be expected to want to keep the world much as it is since on the whole it is organized to their advantage, and those who are out to put themselves in a stronger position to change it, it is important to realize how often and how easily the same 'weakness' of the poor is embodied in their relationships. First World development agencies with much sought-after funds are in a very strong position. They decide who will receive money and who will not. They dictate what sort of work among the poor is good and will have their approval. They judge whether an organization is responsible enough to be trusted with their money or not. They more or less oblige the poor to agree with their policies in order to win their favours. If they choose to operate in a paternalistic and overbearing manner, as they frequently do however politely they do it, they need never take instructions from the poor or be accountable to them in any way. Once again, even though the powerful may be of the benevolent variety, sheep maybe in wolves' clothing, the poor have little if any say over what happens to them.

It is probably an illusion to think that First World development agencies can ever give up this power entirely. Some of their Third World partners will ask them not to do so if it means off-loading even more problems and responsibilities on to them by, for example, asking them to choose between two applications for grants when there is not enough money for both. But if we argue as we do on moral grounds for an attempt to redress the imbalance of power between rich and poor, then moral integrity requires us to face up to the challenge here as everywhere else. Christian First World agencies above all, sharing resources with Third World partners, must look for ways in which those who represent the poor can call the tune, setting the guidelines and priorities for action, deciding how resources which 'belong' as much to them as to anyon else are to be allocated, and asking their First World colleagues for an account of their stewardship.

A SUB-CHRISTIAN END IN VIEW

The charge of being 'sub-Christian' in our thinking about what is good for the poor can be levelled at the apparent 'end' we have in view as well as the means. It falls far short of the Christian vision.

Christians are wise not to spell out in detail all the features of the Kingdom of God or the new heaven and the new earth. Involved with God in a genuinely creative process, we do not yet know what we shall be. Much remains to be discovered about the kind of world or universe which will best satisfy the divine longing and fulfil the potential of all that now exists, ourselves included. There is much to learn. But we are not without ideas and foretastes of what such a world might be like, and some of them have been known to us for a very long time.

For example, in the background of Jesus' early proclamation of a new world (in Luke 4.18f.) where the poor would hear good news, captives find release, the blind see and a more 'acceptable year' would be inaugurated, are very likely not only similar promises made to those who had been exiled from Jerusalem in Babylon (Isaiah 61), but the idea of the Jubilee Year set out in Leviticus 25 where, once in every fifty years, bonded labourers would be freed, property including land redistributed, and debts forgiven. It was a world where somehow strength could never be accumulated in such a way as to permanently overwhelm the weak. Other parts of the biblical tradition present us with idyllic pictures of nature reconciled to itself, the lion resting with the lamb, promising a deeper and more universal reconciliation; or with the prospect of human divisions, whether between Jew and Gentile or male and female or bond and free, being transformed into companionship; or with the hope that the travails of the creation will cease to be occasions for groaning and waiting and be replaced by the security and freedom of the best of family relationships so releasing energies of a quite different kind; or with images of brides and weddings, wine and feasting, hospitable open cities, where misery, including the misery of poverty, is a thing of the past.

All these eschatological ideas and visions of the end or goal or *eschaton* to which everything is or ought to be moving, seem a far cry from attempts to redress the balance and create a world of uneasy confrontation, where strength matches strength and we keep each other at arm's length rather than embrace, eyeing each other nervously and defensively from a distance. It does not even qualify as a just world where at least what is wrong is put right even if there is little love to go with it. Instead of positively striving for the best, we seem content merely to guard against the worst.

Two remarks can once again be made in response to the criticism. First, it is perfectly true that for Christians the desirable moral end goes far beyond the one we are at present setting out to achieve. It is, however, a mistake to see our visions of the end as readily translatable into practical arrangements here and now—a Kingdom of God here on earth. It is worth remembering that none of the visions in the Bible have been realized either in its own time or since. Jubilee was almost certainly never put into practice and even in Leviticus it shows signs of being unworkable in 'urban' areas. Neither Isaiah's nor Jesus' promises were ever fulfilled as social or political realities. Isaiah 61 is in fact addressed to exiles who have returned to Jerusalem and have found it a tough and disappointing experience; and there is worse to come.

The promises of immediate liberation and sight and forgiveness suggested by the astonishing conclusion to the Nazareth sermon: 'Today this scripture has been fulfilled in your hearing' had to be understood as directed to a limited number of individuals if they were to sound at all convincing. Some did see and walk. Jesus was right to reassure John the Baptist that this was so. Some did find release from the prisons of shame and guilt to which others had condemned them, but the larger reality of a shackled and subjugated people, and of social groups cast out beyond the pale, remained as it was. Meanwhile, the nations and the races remain unreconciled after two thousand years. Nature seems to have more reason to groan and complain than ever it did as fears for the environment mount up. The city has become a lonely and inhospitable place for many. The poor grow in numbers.

And we are not entirely surprised that these visions of the end have not been realized. Because we are mortal and have limited abilities, the task is too difficult for us. Because we are perverse and sinful we lack the will for the task. That is not to say that visions have no validity or serve no useful purpose. They belong to the creative side of our nature which goes beyond what is, to imagine what might be as a first step towards making something new. They reflect a proper dissatisfaction with leaving things 'just' as they are. They refuse to allow us to believe for very long that everything possible has been done. They remind us that there is still much to do and they inspire us to do it. They are not, however, the feasibility studies we need if we are to put an end to poverty.

THE VALUE OF DETERMINING OUR OWN VALUES

The second and more fundamental response to the criticism that in fostering a balance of strength we have a sub-Christian moral end in view, takes us back to the value we uncovered at the end of Chapter 2 concerning the importance of giving everyone the opportunity to determine and pursue their own values, not in isolation, for we need to correct and complement each other's limitations and perversities, but on reasonably equal terms so that we are not virtually obliged to accept the values of others, especially of those who have the wherewithal to help or harm or simply ignore us. This value respects both the capacity and the incapacity of the poor to discern and decide for themselves what is good, and also the capacity and incapacity of the rich. Our visions of the Kingdom or of 'the end to which the whole creation moves' may be very convincing to us, wholly compatible with our understanding of Christian values and in our opinion not just good for us, but for everybody else; and we are entitled to argue our case. But we are not entitled to do so unless those who are subjected to our missionary zeal have the opportunity and freedom to argue back or, we might say, are in a strong enough position to say 'No'.

We are not, therefore, denying that in one sense the immediate 'end' in view is 'sub-Christian'. We are, however, setting one moral value quite deliberately against another: what we may value as a good way for human beings to organize their life together with God on the one hand, and the value of all human beings having the opportunity to determine and pursue their own values on the other;

and we are deliberately opting for the second as a higher value. It does not, as a matter of fact, only guard against the worst of injustice by redressing the imbalance of power and preventing the strong from overwhelming the weak. To revert to teleological moral talk about justifying anything as good by looking to the good that will come of it, it can be seen as a precondition of discerning and pursuing the higher good of the Kingdom of God or the new heaven and the new earth. It is a kind of preparation for the best. It is a precondition because we have no real prospect of discerning what that higher good is until all human beings, and not just a few rich and strong ones, have the chance to join in the creative search; and until we can draw on all the wisdom available, perverse and limited as it often is, instead of ignoring or repressing most of it or imposing what little is possessed by some of us on the rest.

REALISM AND LOVE

By holding to a strategy which seeks to strengthen the poor to stand up to those who otherwise will continue to decide against them, we are left with what might be called a heavy dose of prosaic realism. It may not entirely ignore realities like the more generous and creative side to human nature, but it assumes that more often than not people, especially groups of people, will behave badly if given the chance, and it puts forward rather modest ideas about what, for the time being, we should set out to achieve. While such realism can be challenged as sub-Christian, and the challenge should not be too readily dismissed, it can also be commended as an expression of the greatest and most characteristic of all the Christian virtues, namely love.

Love cares sufficiently for the neighbour to will the neighbour's good. It does not merely want it, it sets out determined to secure it. It knows that little good will be brought about by idle dreams and wishful thinking. It may be reckless in the lengths to which it will go. It may spare itself no expense or effort as it persists in its endeavours. It will, however, be careful and calculating in how it proceeds.

Just as love will achieve no good if it adopts techniques of agricultural production or economic aid and development which simply do not work, so it will do more harm than good if it refuses to take the limitations of human nature fully into account. It must deal with things as they are, not as it would like them to be. Such realism is not the opposite or the betrayal of Christian love. It is a way of loving.

In wanting the best for the poor, and working with them to achieve it, how realistic are we prepared to be? Can we, by this means and by that, rid them of their poverty? Is that a realistic expectation? What hope is there of success?

– 5 –

Hope for development

The so-called 'poor' of the world have received a good deal of attention in recent years. There has been a notable outpouring of public generosity. It found its spring in the mid-1980s in television reports of famine in Ethiopia; and it was turned into a flood by the charismatic leadership of a popstar. As a result, millions of pounds were raised and distributed for relief and development. In October 1985 over 20,000 people lobbied the British Parliament with the demand that government policies should also rise to the occasion; while towards the end of the decade almost everyone paid at least lip-service to the importance of environmental or 'Green' issues which, while interesting the rich, have immediate relevance to the prospects of the poor.

All this added up to one of the more heartening chapters in a much longer story. The question we turn now to ask is whether it will ever have a happy ending. What hope of success is there for all our efforts to discern what is good for the poor and bring it about? What is the context or reality within which we work? Can moralists be assured that doing good actually achieves some good and that their moral endeavours, therefore, make sense? What rational expectations can we entertain after careful reflection on what we observe and experience about our world? and how as Christians do we relate these to our faith and above all to our Christian hope? In the light of our present experience and of our belief in a Christlike God, what hope do we have, not in general but for the world we know, which includes the hungry poor we now know better than ever before?

OPTIMISTS AND PESSIMISTS

When first required to take a formal interest in development issues I was frankly astonished by some of the books I read. They breathed a cheerful optimism that I had not met for many a day in the inner city areas of northern England where I had previously worked, and it refreshed my jaded spirit. It was not just the recognition that there is enough food in the world and to spare. It was the kind of 'demythologizing' or 'demystification' of the whole problem of hunger. Wind and weather contributed, but they were not the main causes. The future did not lie in the lap of the gods, beyond human control. The causes could be understood. The solutions were well within our grasp. Resources were available. Crippling poverty could be removed in a generation. The prize of a world free from destitution was waiting to be won.

This cheerful optimism was somewhat qualified in 1985 by an encounter with Willy Brandt, a stalwart campaigner on Third World issues whom I continue to admire for his vision, his political realism and his tenacity. He was launching a new book linking development and disarmament (*World Armament and World Hunger*). Asked whether there had been much progress in North–South relations since the Brandt Report was first issued he frankly admitted that there had not. The book reinforces his judgement, indeed in one extended section (pp. 49ff.) it reports that matters have gone from bad to worse. Such disappointment is not, however, met with despair. Instead there is a certain stoic, worldly wisdom of a politician who has grown used to the slow pace of international negotiations; but there is more: 'I am not without hope', he says, 'Indeed, realistic confidence in our capacity to build a better world for all has been the foundation of my thinking and the motivation of my work.'

Confidence seems to ebb and flow in commentaries on development emanating from ecumenical church circles. Some raise expectations, like John Owusu's report (in *Africa*, first quarter, 1986) on a Recovery for Ghanaian Agriculture.

Indications currently show that Ghana is on its way to freeing itself from hunger and food dependency, thanks to the determination of the people and the enthusiastic support of the government. . . . Cash crops (of cotton, palm oil and cocoa) also saw considerable improvement.

Similar stories can be told of other African countries such as Zimbabwe, once an area of shortage, later an exporter of food.

Other commentators are full of gloom and doom. A survey of the World Council of Churches' involvement in development over twenty years recalls a mood of hope, assurance and enthusiasm in the mid-1960s but comes to a different conclusion in relation to Africa, Asia and Latin America in the 1980s. Even in Western Europe and North America growing numbers of people are excluded by poverty and powerlessness from sharing in the common life. 'This development is repeated and magnified at the global level. The world's poor are on the increase' (WCC/CICARWS, June 1986, 0663A).

The following observations come from a quite different source:

The 'development decades' straddling the 1960s and 1970s have not, obviously, realised their great expectations. There are still some 1,000 million people in the world, predominantly in the South, living at an 'absolute poverty' level which few of us in the North can even imagine, while the average incomes in the richest countries of the world have enjoyed unparalleled growth rates.

The optimism of the 1950s that the need for aid would fall away has been shattered in a number of ways. In most of the poorest countries, economic growth rates have remained extremely low, and real incomes have declined in many countries over the last decade. Aid appears to be needed on an increasing—not reducing—scale both to fill its original role to help raise growth rates and, in addition, to ameliorate the effects of massive external debts, poor returns on investments, and increased reluctance among international banks to lend to lower-income countries. (John Howell, writing in *British Overseas Aid—Anniversary Review*, 1989)

Personal experiences suggest that expectations should be raised, but not too high. In 1986, in Bangladesh, close to the sea in the Bay of Bengal, I was impressed by the courage of women fighting, often literally with their bare hands, to establish themselves on the land. They had to scratch the soil, defying wind and weather, to grow their crops. They had to ward off powerful landowners or their henchmen who came to hinder their work or steal their produce. The women discovered what they could achieve in solidarity with one another. They could improve their lot. Hope was born. They also discovered how doubly difficult it was to move beyond constant battles and ever-present insecurity to more tranquil rhythms of life and work, to turn their fragile hold on the land into a firm grip. It was as much as they could do to maintain their precarious existence; thus their hope was increasingly difficult to sustain.

In the Sahel there was much talk of vegetable gardens. These are fenced-in plots of land; protected from scavenging goats; supplied wherever possible with some water from a deep well; cultivated by the community of village women, giving them productive work in the dry season, nourishing food to supplement a meagre diet, and some surplus to sell in the market. The sight of one garden remains as a powerful, though maybe misleading symbol. It was large, but apparently neglected. Nothing grew except straggling weeds. Elsewhere women had spoken enthusiastically of the advantages their gardens had brought. In another a crop was growing, though I was told it would do the soil no good. Was this one simply overgrown? Had I come at the wrong time? Was there a crucial shortage of pesticides? Had the communal spirit failed? Was the water shortage so acute that it had begun to defeat them? I could but feel ambivalent. It would be wrong to say there were no prospects, but the prospects did not seem all that bright.

One particular incident in Zaïre seemed typical of so much else. A woman explained that she used to sell plastic shoes in the city. Full of initiative she had cut out the middlemen and made regular trips to Italy to buy the shoes herself. On one such trip she had been overwhelmed by the sight of Italy's fields full of food while in her own country they were empty. She determined to change all that. She gave up shoe selling and gathered together a small group of friends who agreed to spend two weeks out of every four farming together in the countryside. The other two weeks would be spent at home in the city. Land was asked for and made available according to custom. Hard work eventually ensured that the land was cleared and cassava and vegetable crops were planted and growing. The women returned from the city to the land just before the harvest to find that everything they had grown had been destroyed—flattened to the ground, trampled down by the herds of cattle owned by President Mobutu which are allowed to roam freely and feed where they will. I was reminded of 'the well-fed cows of Bashan, who ill-treat the weak, oppress the poor' (Amos 4.1) and of the innumerable ways in which those who struggle for life all over the world are so often and readily trampled on and overwhelmed.

SEVEN PROPOSITIONS

Rational expectations as to what can be achieved will vary of course according to the aspects of human poverty and deprivation to which they relate. It is one thing to look forward to the day when hunger is eliminated along with smallpox. It is another to predict the eventual downfall of an oppressive regime which denies whole communities their chance of health and happiness. It is still another to spell out what we expect to achieve and sustain in terms of a new international economic order which pulls up the roots of poverty from the soil of inequitable arrangements for buying and selling one another's goods and services. Some issues seem more straightforward than others. Again it is one thing to talk of particular issues and quite another to talk of underlying patterns of human behaviour which may ensure that similar issues recur. I would venture, however, a general statement of my own expectations in the form of seven propositions. I believe they are rational, because they are based on thoughtful reflection about what I observe and experience, which is not to say they are beyond dispute.

First, I expect we shall put an end to a multitude of specific problems related to poverty. We shall go on curing diseases, like cancer and AIDS, and matching areas of surplus food with areas where there is a deficit, and making deserts blossom like a rose. We have the technical skills to do so.

Second, I expect problems capable of solution to recur. Famine goes and famine comes. One disease is eliminated, another claims its victims. Here we learn to take better care of the earth, there we do it further harm. One unjust regime is removed, another arises. We breed problems as well as solutions. There are losses as well as gains and where we gain we can also lose.

Third, if I expect to be disappointed I also expect to be surprised. There can be unexpected breakthroughs that come like sudden discoveries or revelations or gifts to us and which exceed our dreams.

Fourth, more often than not I expect improvements to come only as the result of patience and persistent hard work over considerable periods of time.

Fifth, I do not expect those concerned for development ever to reach a point where they are totally at a loss and their resources are totally exhausted and there is nothing more that they can do. Further improvements, however hard to win, are always a possibility.

Sixth, we cannot expect to see complete success, or the day when disaster on a grand or even apocalyptic scale can be ruled out.

Seventh, overall I expect humanity to have to live with what I shall call an 'unstable stable state'. We shall see significant changes for better for worse, for richer for poorer, from one generation to the next, and from one place to another. The position is not static, but there will be little variation in the sum total of human happiness and misery. Progress is not ruled out, but irreversible progress most certainly is and the reformers of this world will never be out of work.

These rational expectations apply, I believe, to the work of development right across the board whether we think in terms of the immediate relief of human suffering, or of working with local communities to strengthen their ability to control the quality of their own lives, or of changing unsatisfactory social, political and economic systems. They apply even more so when the interrelatedness of all such efforts is understood.

THE CURE FOR PESSIMISM

I have called these seven propositions 'rational expectations'. They add up to a sensible acknowledgement of what we can look forward to and what we cannot. It is possible, however, to hear them rather differently. They are not so much sensible as profoundly pessimistic. They admit that by taking a narrow, blinkered view we may convince ourselves that we are making progress, but that if we are brave enough to look at the whole, we cannot. The poor are always with us. We may help to make life better for some, but we shall not finally create the human world we long for. Such pessimism can in turn breed a sense of futility. Intelligent partnership with the poor of the world to improve everybody's quality of life begins to lose its point if tomorrow's world will be not much further forward than today's. The nerve of motivation is touched, and that is doubly serious for those who must not only be motivated themselves, but play their part in motivating others.

There are two or three fairly effective instant remedies to hand. One is a sense of duty. To use traditional moral terms it is 'deontological' in that its force seems to lie within itself and not in its chances of success. It is duty for duty's sake, come what may. And it is 'categorical' in that its claims seem impossible to deny. However limited may be our chances of success, I know that hungry people ought to be fed, and that those denied the opportunity to care for themselves and their families and fulfil their own ideals for human life in community should have that opportunity restored. That claim is absolutely clear—at least to me. I cannot doubt it and I cannot silence it. On this moral basis if no other I totally believe in the cause I and scores of others try to uphold.

A second remedy is to marry this sense of duty to the fifth of my seven propositions. We may never be able to achieve everything, but there is always something more we can achieve. The wise will not lay themselves open to too many blasts from the cold winds of doubt which do none of us any good, or to too much speculation as to the ultimate outcome of their efforts. They will put their heads down and get on and do what can be done. They will put their hands to the plough and not look up.

There is a third remedy for any loss of nerve though it is not perhaps so readily available to everyone, and that is the courage and resilience of the poor themselves. Zaïrian women set to work and begin all over again after their crops have been destroyed. The farmer ruined by pest and drought will not give up. The oppressed continue to organize and resist. Many of them apparently believe that they will overcome, and to meet them is less an opportunity to offer them hope than an occasion for receiving it.

For much of the time such remedies meet with some success. The questions are not, however, entirely silenced and they are definitely not answered as to whether both the poor and the duty-bound are whistling in the dark; and it is difficult and may be unhealthy to suppress the need which remains for a framework of understanding or context for our moral endeavours which adds up, and where limited hopes for development born of rational expectations do not blatantly contradict the unlimited hope which is born of Christ.

THE PESSIMISM OF FAITH

Incidentally this apparent contradiction between Christian faith and experience at the level of hope is somewhat ironic when we remember that at the level of pessimism faith and experience seem to be perfectly in tune. There are aspects of Christian faith as we have seen which actually support the view that we should not expect too much. Two of them have to do with traditional Christian teaching about human beings: that they are limited and that they are sinful. Made in the image of God they have enormous creative potential; but being 'man' and not God, they are limited. Their achievements are limited. Their knowledge and understanding are limited. They can never see or comprehend the whole. That is why, in the field of development for example, when experts at the local level of traditional farming and at the more sophisticated level of international economics and aid disagree among themselves and struggle with little success to find agreed solutions to problems, we are not surprised.

What else can you expect from limited human beings coming at it from inevitably partial points of view? And that is why, when they do make headway, nothing they achieve can be regarded as absolute or final. To do so is to turn delight and respect for what we can do into idolatry. Expectations must be limited. We must inevitably be disappointed. We ought, in fact, to be disappointed. In the field of development as in all other fields of human endeavour it is not only important to believe that more can be done, but to insist that more should be done, since any scheme for human fulfilment in community cannot by definition be the last word.

Expectations become even more restrained when we take into account the Christian teaching about sin. Once again it confirms what we observe from experience, but like all doctrine, out of vastly more experience than is available to us. We are not only limited, we are perverse, and often excessively perverse at that. We do not put an end to human deprivation simply because we 'cannot', but because we 'will not'. It is not that we cannot redistribute food. It is not that we cannot redistribute land. It is not that we cannot re-organize the trading arrangements which constantly put Third World countries at a disadvantage. Or at least it is not merely that we cannot. It is that we will not; and two thousand years of Christian missionary activity which not a few have seen in terms of a crusade to free human beings from this 'bondage of the will', do not seem to have made all that noticeable a difference.

This human recalcitrance is not to my mind satisfactorily accounted for by much traditional theology which puts it down to stubborn disobedience. That says far too little about the mystery of a world which so persistently invites and provokes that so-called disobedience, a world which inspires such feelings of threat and insecurity in us that we are constantly driven to make choices which seem to offer us immediate protection rather than those which, in the long run, may be in everybody's best interests including our own. It may in fact be misleading to say that human beings can put an end to human deprivation and can legislate for human happiness, but they will not. Maybe at a deeper level than their limitations they cannot, given the nature of their living conditions. Are they conditions that God has created for God's own strange purposes, or are they conditions which puzzle and oppose God as much as they oppose us?

The links between our ability or lack of it to choose what is good, and the fears and insecurities which encourage our narrow self-interest, are not unrelated to other links, for example between development and disarmament and the way in which any hope for the first derives less from a reduction in what we spend on arms than from a reduction in fear and the creation of a safer and less threatening world where there is less cause to build up our defences and even less to contemplate that the best form of defence might be attack.

Here then are aspects of faith which can foster a lack of hope for development. Our limitations and perversity lower our expectations. But we must turn back our attention to that great central Christian affirmation which encourages us to rob all such pessimism of the last word. What then of our Christian hope as such?

VARIETIES OF CHRISTIAN OPINION ON HOPE

Before we come to our hope, and in particular for the poor of the earth, it is important to remind ourselves of the hopes of others, not, as we shall see, in order to fall into line but to avoid another kind of poverty—often unnecessary—which never considers a wider range of possibilities for believing because it has never heard of them. What then have other Christians, in other times and places, expected?

A cursory glance at Christian history from New Testament times until today reveals how opinions have varied as to (a) the nature of the final outcome of our human pilgrimage; (b) the relation between this world and the world to come; (c) the timing of the 'end'; and (d) the basis for Christian confidence. We look briefly at each of these in turn.

The nature of the final outcome

For most Christians this has involved a sharp and permanent division between heaven and hell, the saved and the damned, sheep and goats, those on God's right hand and those on God's left. A day of reckoning will come and a great gulf will be fixed. Only so can God's righteousness be upheld. Universalism has been a minority view, often regarded as heretical. It maintains that each and everyone will find a place in God's future. If not, then God's love and God's power to win the full response of all creation is denied.

Mediating between such irreconcilables have been various opinions as to the degree to which the future beyond death is open or closed. Where it is absolutely closed, then at death an individual's fate is decided. Where it is opened a little there is some opportunity to repent through purgatorial sufferings. In this way the seeming injustice of unequal opportunities to do God's will on earth is softened. Where the future is more radically open there are no limits to God's endeavours to redeem and fulfil us or to our opportunities to take advantage of them. Death is not the end, only a staging post, and heaven itself is not a point of arrival but the joyful occasion of further creative developments. What makes little progress in this life and seems incapable of achievement, can be advanced in the next.

This world and the next

Of more immediate interest to us are the various Christian opinions as to the relation of this world to the world to come. We may group them into four general types. The first looks forward to the coming of God's future here on earth. History will see God's dreams come true. This world will become God's Kingdom. God's will will be done here, rather than in heaven. This world is the locus of the world to come. Such optimism found expression in the nineteenth-century liberal social gospel and, to some extent, in the more recent secular gospel and the liberation theologies of the mid-twentieth century. It borders on utopianism. It harks back to the Jewish expectation, not of an after-life, but that Israel could look forward to eventual national prosperity, an expectation which broadened out under the influence of the prophets into a more attractive vision of a world of universal peace and justice where God rules over all the nations.

The second type is diametrically opposed to the first. Far from hospitable it is positively hostile to the world that we know and sees no future for it at all. We readily associate it with extreme apocalyptic visions in which, after war and plague and famine and other forms of terrible destruction, God puts an end to the creation. The revival of eschatology in the nineteenth century also spoke of dramatic eruptions into history rather than continuity, and of totally replacing the old order with the new. Hostility to the world has, however, been the rule rather than the exception, characterizing much of the long sweep of Christian history from the days of the early Church through the Middle Ages down to the Enlightenment. It is far from unknown today. More often than not Christians have seen the world as a wicked place and our best and realistic hope has been not to transform it but to survive it, unscathed, with our eyes firmly set on the world above. However good God's original creation and whatever God's original intentions, this world has gone irretrievably wrong. To be saved is to escape.

A third opinion sees a real future for the present world as it is taken up into the world to come. It will not be written off but carried forward. Paul, for example, talks about its transformation. What is sown a fleshly body will be raised a spiritual body. He also speaks of the whole creation watching for its redemption, not just the children of God. The creeds speak of the Resurrection of the Body, not the Immortality of the Soul. Nearer our time, Teilhard de Chardin envisaged a critical point in time at which the present universe would be transfigured. The whole temporal, evolutionary process would give rise to it, like some great reservoir of power finally bursting its banks. God's future does not reject or negate the present world, but is somehow its child. Process theology can also be heard to suggest that the achievements of this present time are not lost but taken up and incorporated into a growing reality to which they contribute.

Some of these ideas linking this world and the next are rooted in convictions about the integral relationship between matter and spirit and between human beings in their psychosomatic unity and the whole of creation. Given such integrity it is difficult to see how there can be personal existence apart from the rest of creation, or how the material or natural world could be cast aside without jeopardizing what appears to be all of a piece.

The fourth and final way of understanding the relation between this world and the next does not agree. It does not despise the present world. Indeed it respects it as having a necessary part to play. But one day its work will be done. It will be outlived and out-grown and left behind. It is not an essential part of God's future even if it is an essential part of God's plan. It may, for example, exist to provide opportunities for the Gospel to be preached, or according to Bultmann, as a place where the individual may at any moment come to the end of an inauthentic existence and begin the life of faith. The individual then has a future; the created order in which he or she is opened up to it does not. A more substantial view of the necessary but temporary role of the world is expressed by theo-logians as old as Irenaeus and as recent as John Hick. This world is the most appropriate environment which can be devised for human development, or at least for one particular phase of it. Once complete, another phase will begin, but it will require a different environment. This world then is like a cradle, or a nursery, or a school, or a chrysalis. It is a vale of soul-making. Nothing could develop without it, but there comes a time when it is appropriately left behind.

The timing of the end
Christian history has not only disagreed about the nature of God's future and the way in which this present world is related to it, it has, in the third place, disagreed about the timing of its coming. When will the end be? Christian apocalyptic echoed the answers of Jewish apocalyptic. The end was imminent and would follow a series of woes and warnings. Christian sects ever since, having read the signs of the times, have predicted that the end was near. Jesus did not apparently approve of such speculation. He said he did not know when the end would come, but, along with the Jews and the early Christians, he thought it would come soon and it was wise to be on the alert and ready for its coming. The early Church had to make considerable adjustments to its thinking and its attitude to life in this world when the expected parousia failed to materialize. Eventually it ahd to settle down and take responsibility for a world to which it felt it did not belong. Two other poinions about the timing of the end should be mentioned. They move us in opposite directions, but they are not incompatible. One looks towards an indefinite future. It is more or less content to affirm that history will be brought to some kind of conclusion, but without saying when. The other looks towards the present.

If the 'last things' are not so much the final things to happen but the most important, just as the 'last word' may not always be the final word spoken but is somehow definitive, then the last things have already happened and are happening now. God has come in Christ. Christ has already returned in the gift of the Spirit. God's will has been done on earth in the obedient life of God's Son. Through his ministry and death and resurrection men and women have experienced the power of redemption. They have already become new creatures. They have inherited eternal life or, not believing, have been condemned already. This was the experience of the early Church, echoed by Paul and John, by demythologizers like Bultmann, by the secular theologians who understood Christianity largely in terms of this present world, and by scholars as varied in their general approach as Karl Barth and C.H. Dodd. They still look to the future, but it is the past and present events which seem to be decisive.

The basis for hope

What is the basis for Christian hope? Two main answers are given to the question and once again they differ. One points to experience while the other, almost in despair, points away from it. The first believes that despite the perplexing ambiguities of our experience of this world which cause us to wonder about the goodness and love and power of God, there are memorable events, public and private, in which that goodness is revealed and confirmed. Notable among them in the Judaeo-Christian tradition are the Exodus from Egypt, the Return from Exile, and the life, death and Resurrection of Jesus Christ followed by the gift of the Spirit. Here God's promises are kept. Here God's faithfulness is amply demonstrated. God will not stand by and allow the story of God's people and God's creation to end in disaster. God acts, and it becomes clear that God acts with power. God's enemies, whether they be Egyptians or Babylonians or fear, hatred, famine, sickness or death or any of the powers of this world, are effectively dealt with, and men and women actually experience God's salvation in their own lives. All this amounts to impressive evidence that, despite the sufferings of this present time, all will eventually be well.

Sometimes, however, those sufferings became almost too great for such beliefs to be sustained. History dealt God's people, Jews and Christians alike, such terrible blows that evidence for God's goodness and power became hard to come by. They must look elsewhere. At such moments, often we should note of bitter persecution, the basis for hope was not inference from experience, but special revelation, or what we refer to as apocalyptic. At such moments it was not life on earth, but 'The Open Heaven', the night visions of a Daniel and the voices and visions of a John on Patmos which became the basis for hope.

In noting as we have done the considerable variety of opinion which surrounds our Christian hope we should also note its virtually unwavering confidence that God is in charge. Some would argue that that is indeed the most important teaching of apocalyptic. Its main concern is not an imminent and catastrophic end to history, but that despite appearances God is still everywhere at work and fully in control. It is the same confidence that allows us to talk of God's Kingdom as eternal, past, present and future. There has never been and will never be a time when God's rule is abdicated or overthrown.

ONE MAN'S FAITH

At this point I can hardly avoid saying something about my own personal faith and hope since it is that which must finally come to terms with my experience and my own rational and, some might say, pessimistic expectations of an 'unstable stable state' in the field of development. This faith of mine does not, as far as I understand it, have to be merely a restatement of traditional Christian beliefs, let alone of New Testament perspectives or teachings, but it does need to take them into account. Christians are not required to believe the same things. They certainly have never done so, as we have seen, and on the basis of what we have noted about human limitations and perversity it is better that they should not. All our formulations of truth are bound in some measure to be wrong. They are formulated from a limited point of view and so fail to see the whole, or take everything into account. They are coloured, some would say largely determined, by self-interest giving prominence to what the formulator finds most congenial (for the better-off, a world which is not likely to change all that much) and dismissing what is less attractive (a radically new order achievable here and now). None of them can be taken as beyond question.

The real Christian error or 'heresy' however is not to get things wrong, since that cannot be avoided, but to get things wrong alone and in isolation from the partial and perverted views of others, past and present, which if listened to may do something to correct and complement our own. That is why, in confessing the hope that is in me, it is important to keep in mind the varied opinions about God's future we have just outlined to save me from unnecessarily narrow and myopic conclusions. And what goes for 'inter-faith dialogue' between Christians also goes, of course, for dialogue between Christians and people of other faiths.

In giving some account of my version of Christian hope, I should make clear that I am describing it. I am not wholly justifying it, indeed I do not think I could; and when I set it out and it enters into dialogue with other versions of faith as it should, it can soon become unsettled. I have no wish, therefore, to claim too much for it. It is simply an account of what is there in me and has come to mean much to me, after some thought of course, and some encounter with experience, and many a dialogue mostly but not entirely within the Christian community.

I should also make clear that this is a faith I do not always hold. Like others I can readily be tripped into agnosticism or another less hopeful 'faith' by the poverty and cruelty and disasters and injustices of life which constantly threaten belief in a good and powerful God; even more so by what strikes me as the sheer insignificance of life once put into a certain perspective. When I think of the space and time scale of the cosmos it seems frankly absurd that our endeavours should add up to anything at all, or that we should worry ourselves about their outcome as I am about to do. Better to make this brief life as tolerable as we can and to be understanding of those who, seeing no such prospect, hope against hope that something more tolerable might follow. I can, of course, rehearse the arguments that counter my agnosticism, but, as for most of us, they do not easily soften the impact of the actual experience when it comes upon me.

What then do I find myself believing when I do believe, and hoping when I hope? My basic belief is in creation not as a 'fact' that once happened or 'thing' once produced by God, but as an 'activity'. Creation is going on. A creative process is under way and I and all human beings are welcome and encouraged to be actively involved. As creative beings with God we are discovering what kind of a world it would be good to make and how actually to make it. That is the basic self-understanding I bring to my work in development. Making a world is what I think of myself along with others as being about.

Like God we are here to work as creators with raw material, chaotic rather than ordered, unformed rather than formed, often presenting itself as threatening and hostile because as yet unmanageable, whether it be the disordered world so persistently marked by disaster, inequality, poverty and oppression, or our own disordered spirits. This is the self-understanding I bring to the seemingly endless hindrances that stand in the way of making a better world. It is not a matter, or mainly a matter, of sorting the good from the bad, the wheat from the tares, and of throwing out, defeating or excluding what is wicked or worthless. It is a matter of taking this raw, chaotic material, of learning how best to live with it, accepting rather than rejecting it, and without approving its disorderly nature, transforming it to take its place in a peaceful universe ordered by love.

Development is part of the work of creation. We proceed, as God has to proceed, by trial and error, since genuine creativity must venture into the unknown and does not know the end at the beginning. Some ideas and experiments in ordering our lives whether, in the development field, they be small-scale agricultural projects, or ways of organizing local co-operatives, or patterns of international trade and mutual dependence, turn out to be promising. They show signs of success. They seem to bring us nearer to the world we had in mind. Others prove to be mistakes and often make the enterprise more difficult. They arouse new fears and insecurities, so that the material we have to work with is even more disordered than before. These risks which creation has to take are amply illustrated by the experience of gains as well as losses in the fight against hunger and poverty, well-known to all development workers, where despite good intentions matters can actually be made worse.

The work is not only risky, it is demanding; it takes time and energy and imagination and patience. It involves sacrifice and generosity. It is an expensive endeavour.

My Christian hope, however, is that, despite the setbacks and despite the cost, the goal of creation will be achieved. The enterprise is risky, painful and demanding, but not abortive. What is being made will be made, though since, as I assume, it will be full of creative possibilities, never finalized. I also hope that nothing will be lost. All the raw material, often made even more recalcitrant by false moves in the creative enterprise, will eventually be fashioned by imaginative and costly love and find its place. In this sense I am a thoroughgoing universalist. All women and men have a place in God's future, as they are and as they can and will become. There is no eternal hell and no moment when any are finally, if sadly, set aside. And not only women and men have a future, but also what we call the natural world to which they are inextricably bound and which seems already to participate in spiritual realities.

There is another sense in which I believe (when I do believe) and hope (when I do hope) that nothing will be lost. All our creative endeavours and experiments to sustain life and make it blossom in community contribute to the eventual outcome. What we now set about doing in the workshop of history: finding ways to satisfy human hunger not only for bread but for fulfilment and freedom and friendship and happiness, will not be a waste of time. It may be lost to tomorrow, indeed it often will, but it will not be lost to eternity. The insights we gain and all we manage to achieve are incorporated in the world to come.

In this sense I am a 'realized eschatologist'. I do not believe that the end (or *eschaton*) is now, but that every now is equi-distant from the end to which the whole creation moves. Every present moment of our lives in which we set out, sometimes unsuccessfully, to discover and build a better world, is equally well-placed to contribute to the glory which is yet to be revealed. The last day is no nearer to it than the first. Today is no further from it than the last. We do not progress along the line of history towards the goal, but in every moment of history—our common history, your history and my history—we can fashion and 'stockpile' resources for the paradise God has set out with us to create.

I suppose I think in terms of two parallel, horizontal lines. One is the line of history and in overall terms it does not progress. The last day, should there be one, is neither more nor less akin to paradise than the first in qualitative terms. The second line represents that world which we have in mind to create with God, unseen as yet, but nevertheless existing, and that line does progress, drawing its ever-growing substance from our costly creative historical work; finding its strength, like sap, from the soil of our imaginative love.

Such an understanding of the relation of this world to some other world knows nothing of the theological confidence trick which excuses us from making every effort or even any effort to get rid of present miseries and transform the earth into something more like God's Kingdom by promising 'pie-in-the-sky-when-you-die' or by dismissing present suffering as entirely unimportant or easily borne in the light of what will one day be enjoyed. It is only by endeavouring with all the strength at our command to redeem the here and now that there is any question of fashioning anything at all of what is still to come. The two are not alternatives, but intrinsic to the same reality.

Earlier we passed under review four areas of thought relating to Christian hope: the nature of the outcome; the relation of this world to the next; the timing of the end; and the basis for confidence. What I have confessed about my own Christian hope can be heard to have opinions about two of them: the nature of the outcome; and the relation of this present world to the created world to come. But little has been said so far about the other two. The timing of the end can be quickly dealt with. I do not believe in any imminent completion of the creative process. Quite the reverse. I expect it to take a very long time. I do believe there is a real possibility of imminent disaster, maybe ecological, maybe nuclear. However, it will have exactly the opposite effect to the old apocalyptic woes. It will not hasten the end or herald it. Such disaster will only delay it. It will not be the moment when God finally gives up on creation and writes it off. It will be yet another occasion, different in scale perhaps though not necessarily in kind, when flood and famine and plague and war prove just how risky is the work of creation and how great are the odds against it, and when in love the creator begins yet again with infinite patience to fashion a future out of disordered raw material.

ONE MAN'S BASIS FOR CONFIDENCE

Turning to the fourth area and the basis for hope and confidence, it should be frankly admitted at the outset that for much of it we need look no further than those rational expectations which arise from thoughtful reflection on what we observe about our world. Indeed, our Christian hopes may do little more than repeat those expectations, having dressed them up in the less prosaic language of faith and theology. Our hopes have less to do with what our world might become than with what it already is. They are, to use some jargon, deeply 'contextual' but not in the best sense of addressing the context or the circumstances in which and about which they speak. Rather they are coloured, even determined by the context, and reflect the circumstances to such an extent that they become not only the occasion of what is said but the substance. Context becomes content.

This is all too obviously true of the liberal social Gospel of the nineteenth century and the secular Gospel of the twentieth century. The liberal hope of a heaven on earth, fashioned out of social, economic, industrial and political institutions redeemed and transformed by love, echoes the understandable optimism of the age. It simply tells us what was expected by Christian and non-Christian alike. The secular Gospel which came close to equating mid-twentieth-century urban life with God's Kingdom, reflects its own (short-lived) confidence as well as its inability, under the philosophical influences of the age, to conceive of a reality other than the one it could touch and see.

Darker and more sombre versions of Christian hope have also been contextual in this way. Apocalyptic and the more staple diet of Christian theology throughout the Middle Ages offer us the promise of a world to come, but it is largely a way of writing off the present world and a commentary on its irredeemable wickedness. It speaks of dark and troubled times when it was unrealistic and unreasonable to expect anything brighter and better. In similar fashion Christians who expect vast numbers of people to go to hell, so admitting a large measure of defeat for God and the Gospel of Jesus Christ, tell us less about the future than the intractable nature of the present. Despite all that is said about the possibility of salvation you cannot expect most people to change.

My own version of Christian hope also finds much of its justification and substance in my rational expectations. It too speaks largely of this world that I know. In trying to confess my hope I have talked about our involvement in the work of creation. I have talked about the real achievements we can make in discovering the character of a world that is good for us all to live in, and in advancing towards it. I have talked about the risks and the setbacks, and the way in which creative experiments can prove to be abortive and disastrous, so that the last state, at least for the time being, is worse that the first. I have talked of the cost of the enterprise and the difficult material with which we have to work. All this adds up to little more than counterpoint to the seven propositions in which, earlier, I indicated my rational expectations. They play the same tune at a slightly different tempo and in a different key.

Only on a fairly narrow though all-important front do we push beyond these rational expectations. For some, for example, it is to predict the return of Christ and an end to history both in the sense of coming to an end and being gathered up to fulfil its true end or purpose. For me, I push beyond my rational expectations when I affirm that our costly, creative endeavours to discover and fashion a world where all of us can be happy and whole do not go for nothing, not even when they are later lost or reversed before our eyes. They are indeed creative, not just fanciful or a waste of time. They do contribute to what God has in mind, to the glory of which we and God have some idea, but which has yet to be revealed. And that created order—referred to variously as the heavenly city, the new Jerusalem, Paradise, the new heaven and the new earth, the Kingdom with its great and universal feast—will most surely come.

What is my basis for saying that: that costly, creative endeavour, of which the efforts of my friends and colleagues in the field of development are very much a part, is not a waste of time, but often in the short term and always in the long term contributes to a growing good! What is my basis for saying that?

Even here I do not think I am all that far from rational expectations. I do not now mean that I am merely repeating in theological language my knowledge of the world as it is. It is not another case where context becomes content. I do mean that my conclusions even at this point are still based on thoughtful reflection on what I observe and experience of this world. They are matters of faith since they cannot be 'proved', but they are not unreasonable. I have two such bases or reasons for the hope which exceeds my rational expectations.

IMMANUEL KANT

For the first I go back for a moment to a sense of moral duty. I said earlier that when efforts to eradicate poverty and hunger and create in place of them a more human world become so problematic that they seem futile, I can readily find motivation in the moral claim which the poor and hungry of the world make upon me. I cannot doubt for one moment that I ought to join with others and try to help, however low my spirits and my expectations.

I have long been a great admirer of the eighteenth-century philosopher Immanuel Kant, though never over-confident that I entirely understood what Kant was saying. However, Kant was also deeply impressed by the moral claim. He also experienced a sense of duty. The Moral Law within said that there were things he ought to do; and he also found it inescapable. With his fundamental confidence in the rationality of human existence, he suggested that such an experience or fact of life carried certain implications. One concerned God; one interestingly enough concerned life after death; but only a third need concern us now. It was that if you had a duty to do good—and he, like me, believed without doubt that we had—then doing good must lead to good results. There could be no force, let alone moral force, about a requirement to act in ways which were simply futile and a waste of time, and it was precisely Kant's experience and mine that the moral claim does have tremendous force. Kant recognized as we do that often our efforts to do good apparently lead nowhere, which is why even such an agnostic as he went on to talk about a life after death, where virtue and happiness would finally coincide, and about a being who would ensure that they did so; but he regarded that as a perfectly rational, legitimate conclusion. We clearly have moral duties and equally clearly there could never be a moral duty to act in entirely pointless ways.

Following Kant, if I have understood him, I have to say that thoughtful reflection on my sense of duty leads to the reasonable conclusion that good will achieve good and that, even if it cannot be said of this world, a world is coming into being where hunger and degradation are no more.

JESUS

But there is a second basis for hope insofar as it is in me, and it adds its weight to the first; just as theologies of revelation at their best have added weight to rather than undermined natural theologies. It not only provides reasonable grounds for expecting that costly endeavour does not go for nothing but actually achieves something in the end, it offers a quite stunning and unforgettable example. It is as hard to dismiss for Christians as the moral claim and its rational implications were hard to dismiss for Kant. It is, of course, the history of Jesus.

Here as I understand it we have not the only case but a quite exemplary case of a man who was obedient to the moral claim as he understood it, within the circumstances of his time and place and the proper limitations of his humanity. He did not always get it right (see for example Matthew 15:21-28; Mark 11:12-14). No human being ever does, but that is not the point. He was exceptionally persistent in doing the good as he saw it. To put it in our own terms he entered fully into God's creative work. He sought to discover what kind of a world it might be worth making. It was often a painful search especially as he broke away from acceptable pecking orders in Jewish society and from a world vision in which Jews remained dominant and from which Gentiles and social rejects were largely excluded. Not only did he seek to discover the kind of world God had in mind, he made every effort to bring it about.

His life in Galilee and Judaea and Jerusalem is the story of that costly endeavour. He feeds the hungry with good things, he heals, he accepts, he challenges, he allows people to grow, he confronts whatever prevents their growth, he himself is challenged and grows, he is generous to the point of sacrifice, and when the storm gathers he braves it out, he suffers and finally he dies. Here is costly creative endeavour that we should all wish to emulate in our own way. Few have managed to do so.

The obvious point to make is that in so many ways his efforts appear to be futile, mirroring the frustration we feel when our own poor efforts seem to get us no further forward. The poor he championed remained poor. The mind of a people which he tried to change remained much as before. He showed them the way that leads to peace. They stuck to their own way and thirty years after his death organized an abortive uprising that was ruthlessly crushed. Twenty centuries later, true to what we have been saying all along, we have still not learnt his way and the world in overall terms can hardly be said to be a more attractive place than before his coming.

Here then is creative endeavour in danger of going for nothing. What else is there to say? Not for me that a miraculous return from the dead put all other rational considerations in the shade. If I ask why we remember the history of Jesus the answer lies for me in the testimony of those who felt the immediate impact of his costly endeavours. They were in no doubt that something quite remarkable had been experienced. They described it in many different ways. Some testified to their release from destructive guilt. For others the fear of death had been overcome. Where there had been no tomorrow there was now a future. Seemingly impossible divides between individuals and communities had been bridged. Seemingly impregnable powers that dictated the character of the world had been threatened. So impressive were their experiences that some even suggested that this man's costly endeavours had inaugurated a new creation. They were new creatures of a new age and they already had an actual foretaste of what the new world would be like. The coming glory had not only been discovered and revealed, but in a fragmentary way possessed.

If my strong sense of moral duty offers me rational grounds for believing that doing good actually does some good, my knowledge of the outcome of the living and dying of Jesus of Nazareth confirms it. Costly endeavour is creative, even though its full achievements cannot be accommodated on our side of dying, or embodied in a world less totally made new than, say, the risen body of Christ.

A GOSPEL MORALITY

If then, in conclusion, I am asked about my hopes for development and whether or not I expect to see a world where hunger and deprivation are no more and we are all free to be well and happy in our various ways, I shall have to stick with the gist of my seven propositions, with their gains and losses and the prospect of an 'unstable stable state'. We have to go on living creatively with a world beset by heartaches and problems rather than slowly but surely seeing them off. We can do much to alleviate human suffering and add to human dignity here and now. We shall never entirely succeed and we shall never be without work to do; but whether we succeed or fail we have not in Christian terms wasted our time. We have contributed now to the happiness and fulfilment which will be hallmarks of the world which is coming into being, in which everything and everyone will find their home. We have in fact more than contributed, for without our hard work in history that world we are making with God could never come about.

To end this book where we began, with the Gospel, such Christian realism, which is neither a false hope nor the denial of any hope, offers yet another example of the relationship between morality and faith. Moral values we said (in Chapter 1) are ultimately statements of faith. They are founded on reason and experience, but also on what we believe. Again any attempt to be moral and to do good can only succeed if it faces up to reality or the real nature of people and of things, including the reality which faith describes. In addition, we can now see how faith can be supportive of morality, sometimes by reminding us of resources beyond our own like the ever-present energies of God, and sometimes, as here, by offering a supportive framework which helps to make sense of our moral endeavours. What 'ought to be' is surrounded and upheld by what, according to the faith of the Gospel, already 'is'.

Too often development—feeding the hungry, lifting up the poor, strengthening the weak, helping God's children to walk in dignity, thirsting after justice—is commended to Christian people exclusively in terms of law. It is their duty. Whether the motive is Christian compassion or good neighbourliness or gratitude for what they themselves have received, they ought to love and serve the poor of the earth. That is true, but it is not enough. Christianity and with it Christian morality is not only about law; it is about the Gospel. It is not only about what ought to be; it is good news about what is the true nature of the case. That news, hard as it may be for us always to believe, is born of our experience of the history of Jesus of Nazareth and of God's history in him and the marvellous creativity of God's costly love. That news is not that you ought to live creatively, as you undoubtedly should, but that life—our life in God's life and God's life in our life—is fundamentally creative. With God we are busy making a world out of all that happens to us in this world and with God it is conceivable that we shall succeed. At the end of the day we shall see the world that we have made, just and festive in its glory, and with God we shall see that it is 'good'.

Notes

Chapter 1 The Gospel and the poor

1 See the helpful though closely argued discussion by Gerard Hughes in his book *Authority in Morals* (Sheed and Ward, 1983).

2 Leviticus 25: see the discussion in John Howard Yoder's *The Politics of Jesus* (Eerdmans, 1972); and above, Chapter 4, pp. 82–3.

3 See Ernesto Cardenal, *The Gospel in Solentiname* (Orbis, 1976); *The Kairos Document* (CIIR and BCC, 1986); *The Road to Damascus* (CIIR and Christian Aid, 1989). *Theology by the People*, ed. Samuel Amirtham and John S. Pobee (WCC, 1986) contains a useful bibliography.

Chapter 2 The value of development

1 This brings us nearer to the classical Christian understanding of conscience: human reason at work on issues of right and wrong, etc.

Chapter 3 Good works

1 Arguments which limit the role of government in promoting social objectives and put considerable faith in the free market system are typical of the 'New Right', which has grown in influence since the 1970s: see R.H. Preston, *Church and Society in the Late Twentieth Century* (SCM, 1983), chapter 3; and J. Philip Wogaman, *Economics and Ethics* (SCM, 1986), chapter 2. Riddell also speaks of 'the view from the Right' (p. 46).

Chapter 4 Strength for the poor

1 See Paulo Freire, *Pedagogy of the Oppressed* (Penguin, 1972).

2 A point expounded in Reinhold Niebuhr's classic book *Moral Man and Immoral Society* (Scribner's, 1960).

Some suggestions for further reading

Samuel Amirtham and John S. Pobee (eds), *Theology by the People* (WCC, 1986)

Banking on the Poor (Christian Aid, 1988)

Willy Brandt, *World Armament and World Hunger* (Gollancz, 1986)

Ernesto Cardenal, *The Gospel in Solentiname* (Maryknoll, NY: Orbis, 1976)

Susan George, *A Fate Worse than Debt* (Penguin, 1988)

Paul Harrison, *The Greening of Africa* (Paladin, 1987)

Brian Hebblethwaite, *The Christian Hope* (Marshall, Morgan and Scott, 1984)

Gerard J. Hughes, *Authority in Morals* (Sheed and Ward, 1983)

The Kairos Document (CIIR and BCC, 1986)

Paul Mosley, *Overseas Aid: its defence and reform* (Wheatsheaf, 1987)

Roger Riddell, *Foreign Aid Reconsidered* (James Currey, 1987)

The Road to Damascus (CIIR and Christian Aid, 1989)

E. F. Schumacher, *Small is Beautiful* (Abacus, 1974)

J. Philip Wogaman, *Economics and Ethics: a Christian enquiry* (SCM, 1986)

John H. Yoder, *The Politics of Jesus* (Eerdmans, 1972)

Index